there's a turkey at your door

More Titles by the Author:

Jacob's Journey
My Morning Cup
Understanding Goose
Fruity Tunes and the Adventures of Rotten Apple

there's a turkey at your door
and other devotional thoughts

Jeanie Shaw

There's a Turkey at Your Door
© 2012 Jeanie Shaw. All rights reserved

No part of this material may be reproduced or transmitted in any form or by any means, electronic or mechanical, including photocopying or recording, or by any information storage or retrieval system, without permission in writing from Jeanie Shaw.

All Scripture quotations, unless indicated, are taken from the NEW INTERNATIONAL VERSION. Copyright ©1973, 1978, 1984 by the International Bible Society. Used by permission of Zondervan Publishing House. All rights reserved.

The "NIV" and "New International Version" trademarks are registered in the United States Patent Trademark Office by the International Bible Society. Use of either trademark requires the permission of the International Bible Society.

Printed in the United States of America
ISBN: 978-1479340125

Cover design: Jennifer Maugel
Interior design: Thais Gloor
Back cover and chapter three photos: Vanessa Embling

www.jeaniesjourneys.com

To three "turkeys" who came to our door:
Kevin, Justin (Gus), and Leigh Ann.

Years before we knew your names we prayed for you—
as we prayed for our children to find spouses who loved God
wholeheartedly and loved our children completely.

You, our sons-in-law and daughter-in-law, are the
perfect answers to those prayers.

I love you deeply and am so grateful for you.

contents

Introduction 11
1. There's a Turkey at Your Door 13
2. Conquering the Black Jeans...16
3. Snapshots of Encouragement 19
4. A Little Encouragement Goes a Long Way.....................22
5. A Century Ride or a Twenty-Five Minute Ride? 24
6. Beware the Critters 27
7. Caller Blocked..30
8. Clarence's Shoe Box 33
9. Deworming the Earworm 36
10. Morphed! 39
11. Sippy Cup Simplicity 41
12. May I Hold Your Emotions? 43
13. Sweetheart, the One-Winged Butterfly 46
14. Life, Interrupted 48
15. In the Curl of the Wave...50
16. Running From the Neighborhood Exhibitionist 53
17. Tangled 56
18. Empty Jars 59
19. Global Roaming 62
20. Caterpillar Killer 65
21. My Solid Rock..68
22. Getting Rid of "Rotten Apple" 70
23. The Particularly Persistent Purple Petunia 73
24. Our Little Mirrors 76

25. From the Sewer 78
26. Old Dog Syndrome 82
27. Almost Taken Out by the Trash Truck 85
28. Carried Close to His Heart 88
29. A Listening Ear 90
30. Good-bye Ol' Friend 93
31. The Circle of Life 98
32. Show Me 101
33. Snippets of Love 104
34. Out of Gas 107
35. Why I Don't Like Fishing 111
36. Erasing "Not Possible" 114
37. What's Your Caption? 117
38. The Power of Music 119
39. Oh, My! What Did I Get Myself Into?! 122
40. Denver's Coming! 125
41. Up Close and Personal 127
42. Leaving a Mark 130
43. The Annoyed Older Brother 133
44. I Can't Hear You! 136
45. Is God Under "They-a"? 138
46. Obedience Is Underrated 141
47. De-Dreading the Dentist 144
48. Kicking Trees 147
49. My, How Things Change! 150
50. The Red *X* 153
51. Troubles and Treasures of Travel 156
52. The Ticket 160
53. An Elephant in the Living Room 163
54. Heart Monitor 166
55. Getting Past the *ABCs* 169
56. The Monitor Told the Truth 173

57. Connection Correction 177
58. Crashing Through the Quitting Places 180
59. Seven Habits for Building a Strong Marriage...................183
60. Falling into Holes...187
61. Dinner with a Friend 190
62. The Day I Was Born 193
63. Getting Unstuck...196
64. Can a Truck Say "Choo Choo"? 199
65. Showing Up 201
66. Walking the Power Lines 204
67. Were Cows Just Here? 208
68. Get Outta My House 211
69. Two Important Words: "Help Me!" 214
70. Dog and Pony Show..218
71. Upstairs Water 221
72. Be Still and—Juggle? 224
73. Closer than a Tick on a Hound Dog 227
74. It's Battle Time! 230
75. Noticing Life 233
76. Filling the Birdfeeder 237
77. A Bird on the Head 240
78. Go Ahead—I'm Covered! 242
79. Team Band-Aid 244
80. Dive In..247
81. Izzy Dizzy 250
82. Painting Papa's Toenails 252
83. Balderdash 254
84. From the Lips of Children 256
85. Another Turkey at the Door! 259
86. The Fellowship of Those Who Encounter Turkeys 261

introduction

As I write the introduction for this book, I am on an airplane, still a few hours away from my destination in Kiev, Ukraine. Although I've been to Kiev a few times, it still feels very unfamiliar to me. My Russian vocabulary consists of two phrases. I remember that the words for *I love you* sound like "yellow blue bus," and *thank you* sounds like a placebo that lives in a hot tub: it's pronounced "spa-cebo." That's the extent of my Russian. So while I'm there, I will need an interpreter in order to communicate. Clearly, Russian is not my first language.

A few weeks ago, I spent some time with a friend I have known since I was four years old. As we spoke about the Bible, she noted that I was fortunate to have been raised with a strong biblical foundation. My dad's friends affectionately called him "the Walking Bible Concordance" because of his ability to recall the Scriptures. My friend added that it seemed as if I had been raised with the Bible as my first language. As I thought about it later, I felt so thankful for the role the Bible has always played in my life.

It's not that faith was automatic for me. I had to do my own searching and studying of the Scriptures to be convinced of many things—I had to come to believe in the Bible's divine inspiration, and become convinced that the Bible has the answers I need for my life! This searching eventually led me to commit my life to Christ during my teen years. The Scriptures have been my guide ever since. As with any "first language," they have become the bedrock through which I interpret and make sense of my life. For this I am deeply grateful.

Even with having such a strong, lifelong foundation in the Word, I realize that in my sinful humanity I can sometimes forget what the Scriptures teach, especially as they apply to my life. I need to be reminded constantly of God's truth. And the Bible has so much more to teach me than I could ever learn in one lifetime—I still have so much more to learn. Several years ago, after writing the book *My Morning Cup* (DPI, 2011), I started writing a blog based on practical, real-life applications of the Scriptures. This blog is a tool I use, not only to share insights in God's word with others, but also to fortify my own convictions and help me make sense of the daily life lessons God offers me. (The blog is called My Morning Cup... Refilled, and you can find it at www.jeaniesjourneys.com.) I have compiled many of these blog posts, along with some new unpublished material, to serve as the chapters in this book. As you read, you will walk with me through a progression of events in my life, just as they unfolded—they are written in the present tense, as I experienced them and learned from them. Throughout these chapters, I have striven to apply the Scriptures to ordinary, everyday happenings of life. This process has helped me to bring God into my minutes, hours, and days, and to transform them from ordinary to extraordinary!

I pray that these pages will serve as a catalyst for your own search and application of the Scriptures. May your Bible knowledge always increase and always inspire. I hope these pages spark within you the desire to make the Scriptures your "mother tongue"—from which you interpret the day-to-day happenings in your life. As the Bible becomes interwoven into your life, I pray that you will also pass on the Bible to your children as their "first language."

In a few hours I will step out of the airport and be immersed in a foreign language. I will need lots of help to do the most basic of tasks. I suppose that if I lived there long enough, I would come to understand the language that now sounds like gibberish to me. Fortunately, the salvation of my soul does not depend upon my understanding of Russian! My salvation does, however, depend on making the Scriptures the foundation for my life.

Join me on this journey to become fluent in God's word.

there's a turkey at your door! 1

On the way home from lunch today, I noticed a visitor at my neighbor's front door. He was patiently waiting, looking as though he had just rung the doorbell while waiting to be invited in. The strange thing about this scene was that the visitor was a turkey.

Yes, a large, ugly turkey! My neighbor had no idea that a turkey was on the other side of her front door, as turkeys don't come calling every day. I laughed as I envisioned her surprise upon opening the door.

The fact is, I can be unaware of what is outside my door at any given moment. For all I know, a turkey could be at my door. We usually don't know what waits on the other side of our front door. The Scriptures speak of several things waiting "behind our doors." Three stand out to me.

Waiting Behind Door Number One: Temptation

> "If you do what is right, will you not be accepted? But if you do not do what is right, sin is crouching at your door; it desires to have you, but you must master it."
> (Genesis 4:7)

Sometimes, temptation that can lead to sin is waiting for us, ready to devour us. It's like finding a skunk, a hyena, or even a lion crouching behind your door. Don't let it in and try to make it your pet. At best, it will stink up your house—at worst, it will destroy you.

> Be self-controlled and alert. Your enemy the devil prowls around like a roaring lion looking for someone to devour. Resist him, standing firm in the faith, because you know that your brothers throughout the world are undergoing the same kind of sufferings. (1 Peter 5:8–9)

I pray to be self-controlled and alert, so I don't open the door to that which can spiritually harm me.

Waiting Behind Door Number Two: Opportunities

Truth be told, opportunities may also be waiting for you outside of your door.

> "Ask and it will be given to you; seek and you will find; knock and the door will be opened to you. For everyone who asks receives; he who seeks finds; and to him who knocks, the door will be opened." (Matthew 7:7–8)

When we inquire of God and seek a relationship with him, he eagerly awaits us. If we fail to seek him or inquire of him, we will miss out on untold blessings and privileges that last through eternity.

> I do not want to see you now and make only a passing visit; I hope to spend some time with you, if the Lord permits. But I will stay on at Ephesus until Pentecost, because a great door for effective work has opened to me, and there are many who oppose me. (1 Corinthians 16:7–9)

Effective opportunities for sharing the amazing promises of Jesus, which can change the course of eternity in people's lives, may also be waiting outside of our door. Again, I must be alert and prayerful to see them.

And Behind Door Number Three: Heaven

> After this I looked, and there before me was a door standing open in heaven. And the voice I had first heard speaking to me like a trumpet said, "Come up here, and I will show you what must take place after this...."
>
> Each of the four living creatures had six wings and was covered with eyes all around, even under his wings. Day and night they never stop saying:
>
> "Holy, holy, holy
> is the Lord God Almighty,
>   who was, and is, and is to come....
>
> "You are worthy, our Lord and God,
>   to receive glory and honor and power,
> for you created all things,
>   and by your will they were created
>   and have their being."(Revelation 4:1, 8, 11)

Sometimes I can miss the big picture, the spiritual reality, which is right in front of me. This can happen most often when I become distracted with the details and busyness of things that won't matter or exist a hundred years from now. I pray that each day my eyes and heart are awakened to the heavenly, spiritual realm that is true reality, and the only thing that really matters.

What is at your front door?

conquering the black jeans

2

I have a job to complete. I'm sitting at my kitchen counter with my Hello Kitty sewing machine, hemming some black jeans. (Yes, I use a Hello Kitty sewing machine. It is simple enough for me to use, and I figured that I could teach my grandkids to sew with it.) I purchased some jeans for my husband about three years ago because they were his size...sort of. I found them on sale for one dollar. Yes, one dollar. The size was not marked, but they looked "about right" for him. They actually did fit him well, except for their length. I think their length was the reason these jeans were on sale. They would have fit well if my husband was about eight and a half feet tall. He is tall, but not that tall! Well, I am happy to report that I just completed the job of hemming those black jeans.

For some reason, I have procrastinated hemming these jeans for the past three years. I'm ashamed to say that they have been folded in the corner of our room the entire time. It actually took me three minutes to get the sewing machine set up with the requisite black thread. It took a few more minutes to hem both pant legs and another minute to put the machine back in the closet. That's it. Three years to actually make the decision to act... which took less than ten minutes to complete.

This new year, I wanted to begin by conquering this silly, crazy thing that had been hanging over my head for much too long. It was eleven o'clock in the evening and I was determined not to let another day pass without facing this project. Another thing I had put off for way too long was taking down a cobweb from the corner of my shower. This job required my getting a footstool and wiping the corner of the shower stall. This was not a big deal, but every day for months I would look up at that corner and say to myself, "I really should do something about this."

Well, I'm happy to say the cobweb is gone. I am quite sure I have spent much more time thinking about "getting around to it" than it actually took to do it. I even experienced what my friend Fred Faller coined "anticipatory fatigue" while thinking about it. I had to come to a point where I decided it was time to act on my good intentions. I said to myself, "If I don't do this today, then when will I... really?"

While these two projects are not really all that important in the big scheme of things, they had gotten the best of me. I just didn't want to do them yet. However, I was always planning to "get around to them."

Putting off until tomorrow can be a dangerous habit, especially if it affects life issues that are of utmost importance. Perhaps you have been thinking of pursuing or strengthening your relationship with God, or changing something that keeps you from following him wholeheartedly. Or maybe you've put off small tasks like the ones mentioned here.

Sometimes, like Felix in the scripture below, we procrastinate because we are afraid of change.

> Several days later Felix came with his wife Drusilla, who was a Jewess. He sent for Paul and listened to him as he spoke about faith in Christ Jesus. As Paul discoursed on righteousness, self-control and the judgment to come, Felix was afraid and said, "That's enough for now! You may leave. When I find it convenient, I will send for you." (Acts 24:24–25)

At other times, it is easy to get complacent, thinking that nothing is really that urgent. The Scriptures soberly speak to this way of thinking.

> "Then he said, 'This is what I'll do. I will tear down my barns and build bigger ones, and there I will store all my grain and my goods. And I'll say to myself, "You have plenty of good things laid up for many years. Take life easy; eat, drink and be merry."'
> "But God said to him, 'You fool! This very night your life will be demanded from you. Then who will get what you have prepared for yourself?'" (Luke 12:18–20)

At any rate, I feel so much better after hemming those "dollar jeans" and wiping away the cobwebs. What are you procrastinating about? Go for it today. It could make the difference for today, this year, or even eternity.

snapshots of encouragement 3

> "I tell you the truth, anyone who will not receive the kingdom of God like a little child will never enter it."
> (Luke 18:17)

Over the Thanksgiving weekend, we gathered for our annual Shaw family photo. As the family grows, this is no small feat to accomplish. In fact, if you look at our picture and see everyone's big smiles, you will have no idea how much time has gone into capturing that one moment. There were the predictable blinks, tears, frustrations, laughs, and distractions before the perfect pose was captured.

While awaiting the photo shoot, I was reminded of God's call for us to encourage one another. This reminder came as I watched a situation unfold between two of my grandchildren. It began with a pout. I believe the snapshot of this pout will say more about my granddaughter's attitude than words can tell. Lexi was not feeling particularly encouraged about the upcoming photo shoot. Can you relate? I can. When we don't want do something, we can often keep our expression from showing our displeasure... but the inside of our heart reveals a pout similar to the one on my granddaughter's face.

We all get stuck at times and need others to encourage us. But our ability to "get happy" can be significantly influenced by having someone who cares enough to notice and encourage us to move forward in a positive way. This is where Micah came to the rescue. He loves his cousin and was genuinely concerned about her unhappiness. So he went to her and spoke with her.

> But encourage one another daily, as long as it is called Today, so that none of you may be hardened by sin's deceitfulness. (Hebrews 3:13)

While Lexi is too little to sin, she was still softened in her heart and attitude by some words from her little cousin. (I didn't hear what he said to her, but whatever it was, it certainly helped.)

I reflected on how much I still have room to grow to become more alert to other people's discouragement, unhappiness, or bitterness (which can lead to hardness of heart). I know that for me, this growth begins by taking the time to consider others above myself.

> Do nothing out of selfish ambition or vain conceit, but in humility consider others better than yourselves. (Philippians 2:3)

Most often my intentions are good, but my busyness can blind me to things that are going on in others' lives.

It takes time and consideration to encourage others. May I be more like my grandchildren—noticing others and taking needed action to encourage them.

> And let us consider how we may spur one another on toward love and good deeds. (Hebrews 10:24)

After the "encouragement encounter," Lexi was immediately ready to go.

I pray to also be quick to respond to the encouragement from others.

a little encouragement goes a long way 4

Every morning, my husband and I feed our dogs. The dogs never cease to thrill at this very predictable feeding routine. Jordan, our fourteen-year-old golden retriever, has always been fed in the basement, where we keep his giant tub of food. (No worries, dog lovers—he owns the rest of the house.) Lately, his arthritic hips have made it difficult for him to maneuver stairs, so we began feeding him upstairs.

Occasionally, he forgets this new routine, and in his eagerness, he scurries downstairs to eat. Then, after eating, he barks—and barks again, thinking he cannot make it back up the stairs. (Yes, I can read my dog's thoughts.) Then I have to stand in the doorway where he can see me. When he feels he can't make the climb, all he needs is for me to look at him and tell him that I'm here and that he can do it.

That's all.

A few times, I've had to go down and walk with him, but most of the time, an encouraging word is all he needs to muster the strength to do something he doesn't think he can do. And the encouragement is not in the words I say, since he can't hear anymore. It's just that I'm there and I care. He understands that fact.

I realize that I can at times be like Jordan, barking about

something I think I can't do. Jordan reminds me that I need to look for ways to encourage people. Their "barking" may mean they need some encouragement.

I tell Jordan he is a great dog and that he can do it. He quits barking, looks at the stairs, and comes right up as if he was years younger.

The Scriptures are full of messages of encouragement. I'll share two of my favorite from the Old Testament and two from the New Testament.

> You hear, O Lord, the desire of the afflicted;
> you encourage them, and you listen to their cry.
> (Psalm 10:17)

> Learn to do right!
> Seek justice,
> encourage the oppressed.
> Defend the cause of the fatherless,
> plead the case of the widow. (Isaiah 1:17)

> But encourage one another daily, as long as it is called Today, so that none of you may be hardened by sin's deceitfulness. (Hebrews 3:13)

> Let us not give up meeting together, as some are in the habit of doing, but let us encourage one another—and all the more as you see the Day approaching.
> (Hebrews 10:25)

It takes courage to live a life pleasing to God. These scriptures, as well as the response from my big dog, remind me of the encouragement I need to give, and the encouragement I need to receive.

a century ride or a twenty-five minute ride? 5

A few days ago when I was on Facebook, I noticed that my friend Erica had completed a century bike ride in Colorado. A century ride goes for at least one hundred miles. This particular ride went through four mountain passes. Erica's ride was particularly inspiring to me because she has lupus.

Two weeks ago, I purchased an old-fashioned Schwinn with one speed and pedal brakes. It had dents in the fender, so I got it for ninety-one dollars. It's a beautiful, light blue, retro-style bicycle—the vision of my dreams when I was young. Being the youngest of four girls, new bicycles were not in the picture for me—or for my sisters. They were simply too expensive.

Yesterday I rode my bicycle for twenty-five minutes to the local elementary school and back. My route had four small hills (which did increase my heart rate). However, I didn't want to ride yesterday. In fact, since it was almost dark when my husband and I went out for our ride, it seemed like a futile endeavor. Those short rides, however, are becoming near daily events and are increasing my strength. Today I rode for forty-five minutes.

Over the years I've learned that in my spiritual life, consistency is key. Reading the Bible consistently helps me discern godliness from worldliness. It keeps me from "fuzzy thinking."

> Anyone who lives on milk, being still an infant, is not acquainted with the teaching about righteousness. But solid food is for the mature, who by constant use have trained themselves to distinguish good from evil.
> (Hebrews 5:13–14)

Long journeys can become realities when they begin with shorter, but consistent, efforts. Perhaps someday I'll do a century ride. But then again, maybe I won't. The encouraging thing to me is that today I got on my bike and began pedaling. I've discovered that I really like to ride. Even the difficult hills are rewarding to conquer, especially when I reach the crest and then can coast for a while. On my first ride I had to get off halfway up a hill and walk. Now I don't have to get off when I'm on that hill. I'm making progress. When we spend consistent time with God, we can build our spiritual character, layer upon layer, by daily training.

> His divine power has given us everything we need for life and godliness through our knowledge of him who called us by his own glory and goodness. Through these he has given us his very great and precious promises, so that through them you may participate in the divine nature and escape the corruption in the world caused by evil desires.
>
> For this very reason, make every effort to add to your faith goodness; and to goodness, knowledge; and to knowledge, self-control; and to self-control, perseverance; and to perseverance, godliness; and to godliness, brotherly kindness; and to brotherly kindness, love.
> (2 Peter 1:3–7)

Sometimes I can get stuck spiritually—it seems there is so much to pray about and so much to learn that it feels overwhelming to begin. I can feel as though I am beginning a century ride when I really just need the consistent twenty-five minute ride. I am grateful that every day I can learn something, pray often, and make progress. I can take my tried and tested route to the schoolyard and back, or explore new routes... as long as I keep pedaling. I just need to keep on pedaling.

beware the critters 6

I'm still recovering from the news of my car's diagnosis as I'm waiting for the repair to be completed. I scheduled an appointment for my car after hearing a rattling noise from the fan that began whenever the heat or air conditioning was turned on. I described it to the mechanic as the noise a card makes when clicking along the spokes of a bicycle. The noise in my car became louder and louder every day. While checking into the service department, I noticed that the mechanic had made the correct notation on his repair order—"car makes a horrible noise!"

I asked him what the repair shop could also do about a raunchy smell in the car. (I had assumed it had something to do with the great amount of rain and the unusually warm weather we had been having.) A year ago, after a fishing adventure my husband had organized, some "fish juice" (from freshly cleaned fish) spilled on the carpet in the back seat. I was not at all thrilled with this rotten smell in my car, and Wyndham lovingly worked

very hard to get rid of the smell. So when my car began smelling like death warmed over, I figured the fish smell had been reactivated by the recent moisture and warmth.

I stared in disbelief as I received the news of my car's diagnosis. It seems a mouse family had made a nest under the hood of my car, near the fan. The initial clicking noise I heard happened when the nesting materials began falling into the area around the fan. However, the loud noise happened when the whole mouse family moved in... let's just say that things really "hit the fan" at this point! And so, sadly, the disgusting smell of death warmed over was not just a metaphor. As the service attendant began describing the problem, I began to feel a bit queasy. Then he handed me a voucher for a complimentary lunch at their café while I waited. Was he kidding? How could I think about eating after what I'd just seen?

Since the car also had a few recalls to be fixed, the dealership offered me the use of a free rental car for the day. As I drove home I thought about the scripture in James 1:12–15:

> Blessed is the man who perseveres under trial, because when he has stood the test, he will receive the crown of life that God has promised to those who love him.
>
> When tempted, no one should say, "God is tempting me." For God cannot be tempted by evil, nor does he tempt anyone; but each one is tempted when, by his own evil desire, he is dragged away and enticed. Then, after desire has conceived, it gives birth to sin; and sin, when it is full-grown, gives birth to death.

Temptation takes all kinds of forms: The temptations to be lazy, stingy, selfish, short-tempered, deceitful, impure, condescending, gossipy, prideful (and the like) approach us every day. It's not sinful to be tempted. It's when we let the temptations start bringing their nesting materials into our hearts and minds that we approach danger. One sin can come in to rest in the nest of our hearts, and then invite its entire family. That's when things start to "hit the fan" in our lives. Unless we clean and disinfect our hearts (like what the mechanics had to do to my Toyota), our life begins to stink!

After hearing of my disgusting car situation, I asked the service attendant how I might avoid this problem in the future. He told me what he does. He suggested I could get a cat (that's not going to happen—I'm a dog lover, but I'm allergic to cats) or I could (as he did) purchase two rubber snakes, put them in the driveway, and park my car over them. He said this would scare the mice away. If I do this, I will need to remember that these are fake snakes (I hate snakes and I'm afraid I might forget that these aren't real!), and will need to warn my family and friends as well.

What I do need to remember is that by keeping my heart and mind on spiritual things, sin won't be able to make its nest in my heart. I want to keep it like that!

> Finally, brothers, whatever is true, whatever is noble, whatever is right, whatever is pure, whatever is lovely, whatever is admirable—if anything is excellent or praiseworthy—think about such things. (Philippians 4:8)

> Submit yourselves, then, to God. Resist the devil, and he will flee from you. Come near to God and he will come near to you. (James 4:7–8)

caller blocked 7

My daughters and I talk on the phone at least once a day. I love talking with them. We talk about fun things with their kids, hard things, simple things, as well as the deep things in our hearts. We laugh, cry, or just enjoy each other's company. It's important to us to stay connected. Several days ago, I hadn't heard from my oldest daughter, Melissa, for several days. I called her the next day, and we had a great conversation. The next evening she called me on my husband's phone and remarked how impossible it had been for her to reach me during the last few days. She had left messages and even sent texts, with no response. Meanwhile, I had received none and wondered why. I couldn't understand, as I was receiving plenty of calls from other people, just not from her. She tried again immediately after our conversation, to no avail. My phone showed no acknowledgment of her call.

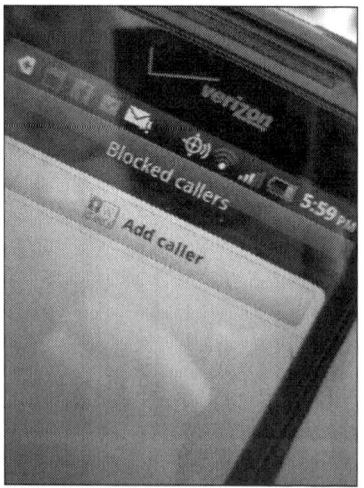

I contacted my cell phone carrier's customer service department and inquired as to the possible cause of the problem. As the representative walked me through "smart phone for dummies" issues, I went to my phone's contact card for my daughter. The problem was clear. Somewhere along the way I must have accidentally checked "block caller." I was so grateful for the representative who showed me how to fix this problem. I called Melissa and we had a good laugh about the experience. I'm freely receiving communication from her once again.

This experience caused me to think about the value of free-flowing communication. It felt terrible and also sad to think that Melissa's communication to me was blocked. I read several scriptures with a deepened understanding—one in the Old Testament, one in the Letters, and one in the Gospels. These are poignant scriptures, and ones I can't forget. Even with God's compassion and tenderness, I mustn't forget his holiness. I never want my sin or hardness of heart to "block" my communication with God.

> Surely the arm of the LORD is not too short to save,
> nor his ear too dull to hear.
> But your iniquities have separated
> you from your God;
> your sins have hidden his face from you,
> so that he will not hear. (Isaiah 59:1–2)

> So I tell you this, and insist on it in the Lord, that you must no longer live as the Gentiles do, in the futility of their thinking. They are darkened in their understanding and separated from the life of God because of the ignorance that is in them due to the hardening of their hearts.
> (Ephesians 4:17–18)

My sin, which Jesus took upon himself while he was on the cross, caused him to experience "blocked calls"—or complete separation from God. He endured that horrific experience so that I can have my sins forgiven and be heard by God himself. What an incredible privilege! I am so grateful to Jesus for giving me the opportunity to have a relationship with God—enabling me to be heard by him.

> And at the ninth hour Jesus cried out in a loud voice, *"Eloi, Eloi, lama sabachthani?"*—which means, "My God, my God, why have you forsaken me?" (Mark 15:34)

My daughter's calls were blocked by an innocent, inadvertent mistake on my part. However, often our "calls" to God are blocked because of our own choices. Sin can block our "calls" to God. This truth hit my heart deeply, when I thought about how painful it would be to have my daughter's calls blocked for real, on purpose.

The separation caused by our sin grieves God. But God's holiness, along with the cost he paid for our sin, demand the separation. Amazingly, God is always eager to forgive us and "unblock" our calls. Jesus provided the means for free-flowing access to God, and is always eager to keep the lines open. May we keep the calls "unblocked" by our pursuit of holiness as we experience God's grace.

Clarence's shoe box — 8

Today, during the staff meeting for our church staff, we had an opportunity to share our appreciation for a dear sister, Laura Webster. It was Laura's birthday, and a big one. An elder's wife, she is a beautiful woman, inside and out. As her strong and burly husband, Clarence, shared about her, he tearfully recounted a story about a shoe box.

As a young man, Clarence had always assumed he would try to create a future by entering the military. One day, his mother (who had became disabled) called him into her room. Under her bed was an old shoe box, which she pulled out to show her son. Upon opening the box and seeing a sea of green, he was dumbfounded  to discover that the box was full of hundred-dollar bills. His mom had saved this money throughout her life. She presented it to Clarence, and implored him to use the money to go to school. He did just that.

It was at the university where Clarence met his wife, who has influenced his life in countless ways—especially when she became a Christian after they got married. Her conversion led to Clarence's own decision to become a Christian. Clarence recently buried his mother, and even more recently his brother, both of whom had become Christians after they learned and obeyed the Scriptures. His sons and daughters-in-law are wonderful Christian men and women as well, and his grandchildren are being raised by faithful, confident parents. So many lives in so many places have been touched by Clarence and Laura. For Clarence, it began with his mother's precious shoe box.

We may never know how an opportunity we give someone can impact their life, as well as the lives of countless other individuals for generations to come. Clarence's mom did not have much money, but she decided to scrimp and save to give her son a chance to succeed. Similarly, I'm reminded of a woman in the Bible whose deeds would be told everywhere the gospel was preached.

> While he was in Bethany, reclining at the table in the home of a man known as Simon the Leper, a woman came with an alabaster jar of very expensive perfume, made of pure nard. She broke the jar and poured the perfume on his head.
>
> Some of those present were saying indignantly to one another, "Why this waste of perfume? It could have been sold for more than a year's wages and the money given to the poor." And they rebuked her harshly.
>
> "Leave her alone," said Jesus. "Why are you bothering her? She has done a beautiful thing to me. The poor you will always have with you, and you can help them any time you want. But you will not always have me. She did what she could. She poured perfume on my body beforehand to prepare for my burial. I tell you the truth, wherever the gospel is preached throughout the world, what she has done will also be told, in memory of her."
> (Mark 14:3–9)

Her sacrificial decision to give "what she could" had a tremendous impact on Jesus and on those who heard of her actions. Even today, centuries later, this woman inspires me to give what I can.

And Clarence's shoe box reminds me that what you and I may be able to give can have a ripple effect of good that may make an eternal difference in many lives—in ways that we may never even see.

> Sow your seed in the morning,
>   and at evening let not your hands be idle,
> for you do not know which will succeed,
>   whether this or that,
>   or whether both will do equally well. (Ecclesiastes 11:6)

deworming the earworm   9

Eeeew! This is my reaction to this disgusting-sounding title. However, this chapter is not really about slimy creatures living inside the crevices of our inner ears or about long squiggly worms cascading down from the openings in our ears.

Earworm is a word coined within the last decade, used to describe catchy phrases, jingles, or songs that get stuck in our minds and replayed over and over (and over) again. Several recent happenings brought earworms to my attention. One is an article I read yesterday, while in the Zurich airport, in a magazine entitled *Hear the World*. (My mother was deaf for the last twenty years of her life, so articles about hearing often catch my attention.) This particular article was about earworms: what causes them (they don't know), and ways to get rid of them.

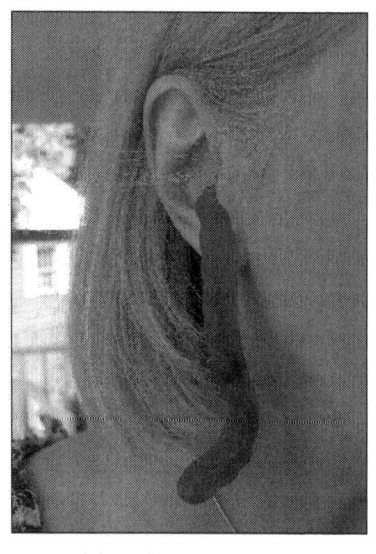

This past weekend my oldest granddaughter, who was visiting us, began to sing a jingle from an advertisement for a jewelry store—"Every kiss begins with Kay." As she was singing I began to randomly say the word "Kay," then give a kiss to her younger sister (who was sitting on my lap) each time I said the word. This brought on laughter, which brought on more spoken "Kays," followed by more kisses. Unfortunately, I was left singing this little ditty in my head all day long.

Now that I have mentioned it, if you are familiar with the song, I may have just passed this annoyance on to you. Similarly, if I were to write a paragraph encouraging you not to think about a red airplane—but then kept repeating instructions, "Don't think about a red airplane"—chances are, you would have a red airplane clearly pictured in your mind.

I read in the magazine article that studies show that the best solution for ridding our minds of earworms is to sing a different song or say another phrase. The Scriptures have always taught this God-given principle. A scripture that has become an oft-used tool for me is found in Romans 12:21. It simply states, "Do not be overcome by evil, but overcome evil with good."

Another scripture that teaches this principle is in Matthew 12:43–45:

> "When an evil spirit comes out of a man, it goes through arid places seeking rest and does not find it. Then it says, 'I will return to the house I left.' When it arrives, it finds the house unoccupied, swept clean and put in order. Then it goes and takes with it seven other spirits more wicked than itself, and they go in and live there. And the final condition of that man is worse than the first."

When I have an unrighteous thought, word, or attitude come into my head, I can be sure it will want to "take up residence" in my heart. I can let it fester and take root, or I can decide (with the help of God) to send it away. These scriptures teach me that, just like the earworms, I won't be able to get rid of these thoughts, words, or attitudes just by thinking about getting them out of my head. Instead, I need to replace them with something else, such as what is described in Philippians 4:8:

> Finally, brothers, whatever is true, whatever is noble, whatever is right, whatever is pure, whatever is lovely, whatever

is admirable—if anything is excellent or praiseworthy—
think about such things.

When I keep scriptures, songs, and righteous "good thoughts" in my "memory arsenal," they prove again and again to be the antidotes for the "sinworms" that can take me captive. These "sinworms" are far more destructive than "earworms"—which can just be annoying.

Either way, I never have liked worms.

morphed! 10

I've always admired close-up pictures of butterflies that "some people" are able to capture in photographs. Well, yesterday was my day. I was "some people." While on a prayer walk, I spied this beautiful creature enjoying some sweet nectar. Butterflies always remind me of the amazing changes that happen while they transform from worm-like creatures into graceful, fluttering specimens of God's handiwork. I carried in my mind a scripture with me throughout the day today. It reads,

> "You diligently study the Scriptures because you think that by them you possess eternal life. These are the Scriptures that testify about me, yet you refuse to come to me to have life." (John 5:39–40)

The Message Bible puts it like this:

> "You have your heads in your Bibles constantly because you think you'll find eternal life there. But you miss the forest for the trees. These Scriptures are all about me! And here I am, standing right before you, and you aren't willing to receive from me the life you say you want."

When I was still more in the "worm" stage of my Christian walk, the Scriptures were important to me. However, they were too often more like something I read to "learn how to do the right thing," rather than something I read because I valued and wanted to bask in the relationship to which they led me. I did learn, however, that even when my understanding was shallow it was still always better to just "do the right thing."

When I was a kid I wanted to be able to tell my Sunday school teacher that I was a DBR—a Daily Bible Reader. She had said we could read verses each day, or just say some from memory in order to be a DBR. So... on some days, I would lay my head on my pillow at the end of the day and remember that I had forgotten to read my Bible. In order to be a "good Bible student" I would quote to myself, "Jesus wept."

Voilà, I was a Daily Bible Reader!

Wow. I'm embarrassed to write that pathetic pharisaical confession. I'm glad the worm has morphed from those days!

As I continued on my prayer walk the other day, I marveled in the delightful reality that I get to walk and talk with my best friend—the creator of the universe, the Almighty God, MY Wonderful Counselor, Prince of Peace, and Lord of Lords... and amazingly, he tells me that he is delighted to hear from me. Utterly delighted. It's hard to fathom, but it's true. And to top it off, as I came to the end of the path I came upon this majestic scene.

And guess what? My Father owns this ocean and made it for my pleasure. On very few days am I able to see this kind of scenery on a prayer walk. This is not the norm for my walks. However, I'm grateful that my relationship with God is not dependent upon the scenery or circumstance. I don't want to miss the forest for the trees. I don't want to just put my head in my Bible—I want to put in my whole heart! It leads me to the most fulfilling, amazing relationship possible.

sippy cup simplicity   11

I often like to think about children. I enjoy teaching them and enjoy being taught by them. Today I was taught by a child. This morning I took my prayer walk with my eighteen-month-old grandson. He listened attentively as I prayed aloud, and occasionally turned to ask me the question, "All done?" It occurred to me how wonderfully refreshing it was to pray in a way that a toddler could comprehend. We thanked God for the beautiful things we saw and asked him to mold our hearts and to be with us in all the things planned for our day. We enjoyed the things God made, and prayed for some specific people. It was pretty straightforward—heartfelt and very simple. (Our singing this morning was perhaps not the most spiritual, as it mainly centered around "The Wheels on the Bus," his personal favorite.) It was a good prayer time; I think God heard us.

Last night after midweek I went with a friend to get ice cream (actually, it was frozen yogurt, my attempt to be more health-conscious—never mind the chopped up Heath Bar mixed in). She was telling me about the simple world of her special-needs son, and sharing her contrasting feelings: Some days she feels she has a very difficult lot in life, while at other times she feels grateful that she has been given a special, secret insight into the joys of life, learning to feel and notice things in a way that she would not without the "tutoring" from her special-needs son. I thought of this scripture:

> "Therefore I tell you, do not worry about your life, what you will eat or drink; or about your body, what you will wear. Is not life more important than food, and the body more important than clothes? Look at the birds of the air; they do not sow or reap or store away in barns, and yet your heavenly Father feeds them. Are you not much more valuable than they? Who of you by worrying can add a single hour to his life?
>
> "And why do you worry about clothes? See how the lilies of the field grow. They do not labor or spin. Yet I tell you that not even Solomon in all his splendor was dressed like one of these. If that is how God clothes the grass of the field, which is here today and tomorrow is thrown into the fire, will he not much more clothe you, O you of little faith? So do not worry, saying, 'What shall we eat?' or 'What shall we drink?' or 'What shall we wear?' For the pagans run after all these things, and your heavenly Father knows that you need them. But seek first his kingdom and his righteousness, and all these things will be given to you as well. Therefore do not worry about tomorrow, for tomorrow will worry about itself. Each day has enough trouble of its own." (Matthew 6:25–34)

If I can just live out the profound childlike simplicity of this verse today, it will be a simply wonderful day.

may I hold your emotions? 12

If you look carefully inside my hands, you may see my oldest grandson's emotions!

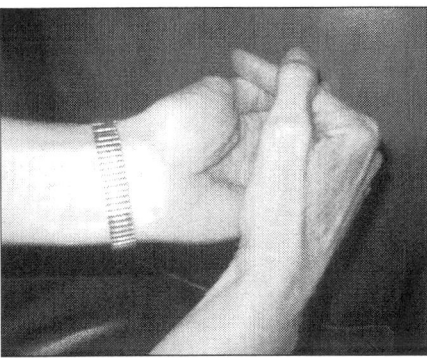

I met my daughter Melissa at the mall yesterday during lunchtime in order to help her with her kids. They were scheduled to have their pictures taken. We played a bit while waiting for their noontime appointment. We waited and we waited some more. About twenty-five minutes later, as Caleb was moving one of the large stools in the waiting area, it slipped and landed on his foot, scraping some skin from his toe. He fell to the ground sobbing, landing on something gooey in the carpet—which promptly stained his freshly laundered khaki shorts. Of course, at this very moment we were called to the room for the photo session.

Things sort of melted down at this point. Caleb was crying and felt his toe was hurting too badly for him to walk. The situation was looking bleak for getting a picture that would contain any smiles. Melissa was doing a great job of comforting him, as well as reminding him of the Chick-fil-A lunch and cupcake dessert that awaited him on the other side of the picture-taking. It seemed that all begging and bribing would be to no avail.

As emotions were flying, I thought of one of my favorite

scriptures—2 Corinthians 10:5. Certainly now was an opportune time to capture some of these emotions.

> We demolish arguments and every pretension that sets itself up against the knowledge of God, and we take captive every thought to make it obedient to Christ.

The Spirit was surely at work at this moment. Remembering the scripture, I cupped my hands and walked over to Caleb. I told him that I would like to hold something for him while he got his picture taken. I wanted to hold his sad emotions and the pain from his foot. I would hold it carefully, and then when he was done I could give it back to him. Amazingly, Caleb put his little hand in between my hands as if to place his emotions inside. Then, an amazing thing happened! He stepped onto the mat where the girls were already standing, posed for a group picture, and gave us all the most beautiful smile imaginable. He could not have been more cooperative or enthusiastic throughout the session. When it was over, I told him how proud I was of him for giving over his emotions and that he could have them back if he wanted. He didn't reach for them.

Later, he told his mom how hard it had been for him to control his emotions when he got hurt. He said that he just couldn't figure out how to get it back together, and was so glad that Nana was there and offered to hold his emotions in her hands. And then he proudly told her that after the pictures were over, he didn't even feel the need to take them back anymore! Melissa and I were amazed that this worked.

However, it's really not that complicated. You see, Caleb really believed that I was capable of taking his emotions, and reliable enough to keep them for him. Again, I am learning from children. If I really believe that God is capable enough and reliable enough to be entrusted with my emotions... I can let go and be at peace! Thank you for this lesson, Caleb.

Do not be anxious about anything, but in everything, by prayer and petition, with thanksgiving, present your requests to God. And the peace of God, which transcends all understanding, will guard your hearts and your minds in Christ Jesus. (Philippians 4:6–7)

Humble yourselves, therefore, under God's mighty hand, that he may lift you up in due time. Cast all your anxiety on him because he cares for you. (1 Peter 5:6–7)

Sweetheart, the one-winged butterfly   13

Yesterday was a heavy-hearted day. A dear friend lost her sister. Another friend lost his mom. Last night, I drove my husband to the airport after receiving word of his father's dire condition after suffering a heart attack. Three of my husband's sisters have had surgeries or hospitalization for illnesses over the last month. Another friend is having trials in her marriage. A scripture in John 16:33 came to mind: "I have told you these things, so that in me you may have peace. In this world you will have trouble." This is quite true. In this world we will have trouble. However, this verse continues: "But take heart! I have overcome the world."

One recent Friday night (we call it Nana and Papa Night), I was privileged to meet a butterfly named Sweetheart. My eight-year-old granddaughter, Emma, brought her over to our house to continue to care for her. About three weeks earlier, our deeply compassionate granddaughter had found the injured little insect on the  ground. Noticing that it had only one wing and could not fly, Emma brought it inside and made it a home in a Tupperware container. She named her "Sweetheart" and surrounded her (Emma somehow knows that the butterfly is a girl) with grass, twigs, and other plants that she learned were pleasing to butterflies. Every day she takes her outside to drink sweet nectar from a "butterfly bush." This little butterfly has already outlived its normal life expectancy. It has survived, and dare I say thrived (even living with one wing and sitting in a Tupperware container), because of the tender compassion of my granddaughter. As I think of my own trials, and as I pray for friends who are hurting today, I picture one-winged Sweetheart being gently lifted onto the nourishment-giving nectar of the butterfly bush. And she keeps on going. I then remember one of my favorite scriptures:

> See, the Sovereign LORD comes with power,
>   and his arm rules for him.
> See, his reward is with him,
>   and his recompense accompanies him.
> He tends his flock like a shepherd:
>   He gathers the lambs in his arms
> and carries them close to his heart;
>   he gently leads those that have young.
> (Isaiah 40:10–11)

Some days I feel a bit like Sweetheart, and need to be helped to find the healing nectar from God. Other days, I just need to be more alert, aware, and compassionate toward those who need help to find their "butterfly bushes."

Whether or not we are able to "fly" today, or feel as though we have a broken wing, may we all feel the strong arms of our Father's compassion—and thrive. And may we be more like Emma by noticing those who need to feel God's compassion through our touch.

life, interrupted   14

Don't you just relish this familiar phone call scenario: The phone is picked up, but before you can even say hello, you are placed on hold? Sometimes it's for a short time, sometimes for a long time, sometimes you get disconnected, and you may even be forgotten. It's not my favorite scenario!

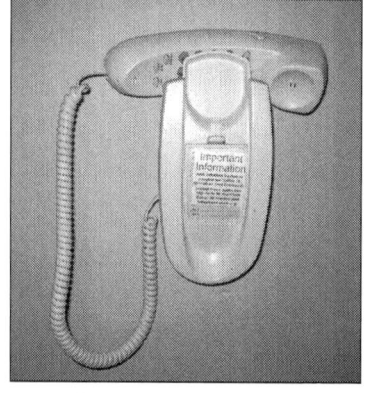

We had lots of plans this week—beginning yesterday with a cookout at our house, and then later today we had planned to spend a few days away with some friends who are flying in from California. Their tickets are non-refundable and can't be changed. This visit has been planned for months. But our plans changed. The stack of burger buns still lines my counter, and there is a shelf stacked with ground beef in the refrigerator. Our plans were interrupted.

We canceled our cookout. While I still plan to pick up our friends from the airport, Wyndham will not be with us. He spent the night in the hospital in Florida with his critically ill father. His dad's condition continues to deteriorate, and he is no longer conscious. Now we wait. As I walked and prayed this morning, several scriptures ran through my mind. The first was this:

> In his heart a man plans his course,
>   but the LORD determines his steps. (Proverbs 16:9)

In fact, Proverbs 16 is filled with wisdom about plans. My plans are not that important compared to the big picture of life. It took a prayer walk to become surrendered to this fact, however. I'm helped by what we call the Lord's Prayer:

> "Give us today our daily bread." (Matthew 6:11)

I'm reminded that the Israelites gathered manna for only one day (except when gathering enough for the Sabbath as well).
Jesus teaches me in Matthew 6:34:

> "Therefore do not worry about tomorrow, for tomorrow will worry about itself. Each day has enough trouble of its own."

I will pray to live today well. That's all I can really plan for. And actually, even the day is broken down into minutes and seconds. That's sort of encouraging. Right now, I can choose to be surrendered to God. I can choose the hope, joy, peace, and comfort that he offers me. Aaahhh. Sweet surrender... at least at this moment. I will probably have to revisit this prayer and these scriptures throughout the day.

I am confident that although I may be on hold, God will not forget me or hang up on me.

> "Can a mother forget the baby at her breast
>   and have no compassion on the child she has
>   borne?
> Though she may forget,
>   I will not forget you!" (Isaiah 49:15)

> God is not unjust; he will not forget your work and the love you have shown him as you have helped his people and continue to help them. (Hebrews 6:10)

in the curl of the wave   15

Wyndham and I went on a prayer walk this morning. Feeling sad about the impending loss of his dad, we felt the urgent need to pray. Since we are staying near an ocean, we went there. As we prayed, the waves were particularly high and loud. As I watched the waves crest, I focused on the curl inside of  the wave and many memories flooded my mind.

I hold a treasured memory of riding waves with my dad when I was a young girl. Having grown up on an island, Dad spent a lot of time in the water. He taught me to ride the waves, which I loved doing. I still enjoy it. I remember the lessons he taught me as he showed me how to find the "sweet spot" in the curl of the wave. He reminded me to keep my hands outstretched as I got caught up in the curl—and to allow the power of the wave to take me to shore. If I got in at just the right place, one wave could take me all the way to the shore. He had this down to a fine art. I was amazed at how far the waves would take him.

As I stood there watching the waves and remembering my dad, I was struck by two things. One was the bigness of God compared to my insignificance... and yet, somehow, God thinks I am significant. As I stood there feeling so small, I remembered Psalm 8:3–5:

> When I consider your heavens,
>> the work of your fingers,
> the moon and the stars,
>> which you have set in place,
> what is man that you are mindful of him,
>> the son of man that you care for him?
> You made him a little lower than the heavenly beings
>> and crowned him with glory and honor.

Just then, several small birds flew overhead, also reminding me of the significance God places on me. It seems unfathomable.

> "Are not two sparrows sold for a penny? Yet not one of them will fall to the ground apart from the will of your Father. And even the very hairs of your head are all numbered. So don't be afraid; you are worth more than many sparrows." (Matthew 10:29–31)

Feeling the sorrow of losing my father-in-law brought me back to the times with my dad, who I had lost several years ago. In my mind's eye, again I could picture the exuberant rush in catching the power of the wave that carried me to the shore. I could almost feel the water rushing over my head and beside me, forcing me toward the shore—all the while tucked into the power of the curl. That, to me, is what it feels like to be tucked inside of the shadow of God's arms.

> Your love, O LORD, reaches to the heavens,
>> your faithfulness to the skies.
> Your righteousness is like the mighty mountains,
>> your justice like the great deep.
> O LORD, you preserve both man and beast.
>> How priceless is your unfailing love!
> Both high and low among men
>> find refuge in the shadow of your wings. (Psalm 36:5–7)

To me, the following Psalm perfectly describes the power of God as can be felt in the curl of the wave. I want to know him, to continue to feel the protection of his arms—and to know and reflect his mighty power!

> The seas have lifted up, O Lord,
> > the seas have lifted up their voice;
> > the seas have lifted up their pounding waves.
>
> Mightier than the thunder of the great waters,
> > mightier than the breakers of the sea—
> > the Lord on high is mighty.
>
> Your statutes stand firm;
> > holiness adorns your house
> > for endless days, O Lord. (Psalm 93:3–5)

running from the neighborhood exhibitionist

16

Yes, that's right. The neighborhood I grew up in had an exhibitionist. I found out because of an afternoon skateboarding adventure. Those of you who read *My Morning Cup* will not be surprised to hear of this experience—it sort of goes with the flow of my life.

As a preteen or young teen (it was a long time ago; I can't remember my age at the time), I was eager to learn to skateboard. Back then, the devices we used were called "turfboards," and most

were handmade. I persuaded my dad to make me one. He took a plank of wood (which I painted and decorated), and then he lovingly attached skate wheels to the bottom of the board. Voilà! My wonderful turfboard was born.

I discovered that the best place to practice my skills was in our neighbor's driveway, across from the pond that was in our back yard. So one afternoon I took my new board and practiced my "moves" over and over again. As I was walking back up my neighbor's driveway, facing the house across the street, a man was standing outstretched behind his picture window—in all his naked glory (or lack thereof). I had three sisters—no brothers. This was a man. This view scared the bejeebies out of me (definition of bejeebies: emotions inside of you that, when activated, cause massive freak-out).

I did not "stop to pass go." I ran and ran and ran. I told my mother what I'd just witnessed, and she then reported it to the police. I have no idea what happened after that. I just know that I never practiced in that driveway again, or walked down that street alone.

I've been thinking about doing some running lately, and it reminded me what it felt like to run in order to get away from something! Yesterday I did some running in order to get to the bank before it closed.

The Scriptures have a lot to say about running. Here are a few about running *toward* something and running *from* something. These scriptures strengthen and challenge me:

> Do you not know that in a race all the runners run, but only one gets the prize? Run in such a way as to get the prize. (1 Corinthians 9:24)

> Therefore I do not run like a man running aimlessly; I do not fight like a man beating the air. No, I beat my body and make it my slave so that after I have preached to others, I myself will not be disqualified for the prize. (1 Corinthians 9:26–27)

> Therefore, since we are surrounded by such a great cloud of witnesses, let us throw off everything that hinders and the sin that so easily entangles, and let us run with perseverance the race marked out for us. (Hebrews 12:1)

> Flee the evil desires of youth, and pursue righteousness, faith, love and peace, along with those who call on the Lord out of a pure heart. (2 Timothy 2:22)

> Submit yourselves, then, to God. Resist the devil, and he will flee from you. (James 4:7)

Years ago I ran hard to get away from the exhibitionist. Ask yourself as I ask myself: How hard do I run from things that aren't good for me or that will distance me from God?

Yesterday I ran hard to get to the bank before it closed. Ask yourself as I ask myself: How eagerly and purposefully will I run toward God and his will for my life today?

tangled 17

I was sitting on the pier at sunset while my husband was casting a line. We were in Jacksonville, Florida, for the funeral of my father-in-law. Wyndham has many memories of times shared with his dad as they fished from that pier.

As a person who doesn't like to smell, touch, or catch fish (although I do like to eat them), I sat on the pier, planning to have some worship time through music. Overhead, the clouds carried vibrant shades of pink, orange, red, and blue. I'm sure it was beautiful... as I did take a picture. However, I had a problem. As I pulled my iPod out and turned to my "Quiet Time playlist," I realized that my earphones  were completely tangled. I don't know how they got contorted into such an intricate knot, but they did.

I felt frustrated, and began a valiant effort to untangle the earphones. It took a while. Several moments after I finished, Wyndham had pulled his line out of the water and was ready to go back to the shore. The setting was beautiful, and the song shuffling through at the time (which I only heard half of) was "It Is Well with My Soul," which starts out, "When peace like a river..." How ironic. I almost completely missed the moment because I'd been so busy untangling my gadget that I never got to listen to the music or watch the sunset. Around me the waves were crashing and the sunset was brilliant—shouting out God's glory. But all the while, I was distracted, trying to get my act together in order to enjoy a peaceful time. I thought of two scriptures  that seemed very applicable. The first was John 5:39:

> You diligently study the Scriptures because you think that by them you possess eternal life. These are the Scriptures that testify about me.

I don't want to ever miss my fellowship with God, even while in the midst of spiritual activity.

The second was Matthew 13:13–17:

> "This is why I speak to them in parables:
>
> 'Though seeing, they do not see;
>   though hearing, they do not hear or understand.'
>
> In them is fulfilled the prophecy of Isaiah:
>
> "'You will be ever hearing but never understanding;
>   you will be ever seeing but never perceiving.
> For this people's heart has become calloused;
>   they hardly hear with their ears,
>   and they have closed their eyes.
> Otherwise they might see with their eyes,
>   hear with their ears,
>   understand with their hearts
> and turn, and I would heal them.'
>
> But blessed are your eyes because they see, and your ears because they hear.
>   For I tell you the truth, many prophets and righteous

men longed to see what you see but did not see it, and to hear what you hear but did not hear it."

Lord, please don't let me get tangled in my focus, so that I miss the things you want me to see, hear, and act upon.

empty jars   18

We buried my father-in-law Saturday. He had been our last living parent. It was a difficult few weeks for our family as his life left his physical body. I felt honored to be there as he breathed his last breath. He passed peacefully, and was appropriately honored. I will miss him.

Difficult times often completely sap our energy. Wyndham and I returned home Sunday feeling exhausted and a bit numb. It seemed hard to reengage in activity here, though we knew we would need to do so soon. I realized it's also been a while since I've written or wanted to write. I felt the reality of a little poem I once read:

> Can't think.
> Brain dumb.
> Inspiration won't come.
> Poor ink, bum pen.
> Best wishes.
> Amen.

I just felt like I didn't have a lot to give.

I went to my Bible, where I knew I could regain my focus. As I was reading from the book of John a scripture ministered to me, and I hope it will encourage you as well.

> On the third day a wedding took place at Cana in Galilee. Jesus' mother was there, and Jesus and his disciples had also been invited to the wedding. When the wine was gone, Jesus' mother said to him, "They have no more wine."

"Dear woman, why do you involve me?" Jesus replied. "My time has not yet come."

His mother said to the servants, "Do whatever he tells you."

Nearby stood six stone water jars, the kind used by the Jews for ceremonial washing, each holding from twenty to thirty gallons.

Jesus said to the servants, "Fill the jars with water"; so they filled them to the brim.

Then he told them, "Now draw some out and take it to the master of the banquet."

They did so, and the master of the banquet tasted the water that had been turned into wine. He did not realize where it had come from, though the servants who had drawn the water knew. Then he called the bridegroom aside and said, "Everyone brings out the choice wine first and then the cheaper wine after the guests have had too much to drink; but you have saved the best till now." (John 2:1-10)

I realize that I have felt sort of like an empty stone water jar. So I took the lesson from Mary, Jesus' mother, and asked Jesus to be involved with my jar. I asked him to refill my jar—spiritually. Though the jars Jesus filled began with nothing and were then filled with water, he turned that water into the finest of wine... his first miracle. I have often felt that resurgence of Jesus' presence in my heart through his Spirit. I delved into his word and asked him for the energy that he powerfully inspires within me as I try to do his will. He promises it. He delivers. I am so grateful!

It is he whom we proclaim, warning everyone and teaching everyone in all wisdom, so that we may present everyone mature in Christ. For this I toil and struggle with all the energy that he powerfully inspires within me.
(Colossians 1:28–29, NRSV)

global roaming 19

This week my work has taken me out of the country. As I prepared for my travels, I learned I needed to change a few settings on my phone in order to avoid exorbitant data roaming fees. I also programmed settings that would allow me to make calls and send and receive texts via global roaming (all for a slight fee). The fact that I can text a message to someone in a far-off country involves sound waves and laws of physics and nature that some very smart people have learned how to use. (And if I used the fancy apps available, I could even press another button that would translate what I wrote into another language!) Understanding how all this works, to me, is like understanding another dimension. Some things just boggle my mind. I can somewhat begin to grasp how this functions, but can't even begin to fathom the "whys" behind the "hows." The laws of physics that must be harnessed, used, and relied upon to make these things work are too wonderful to me.

We had breakfast yesterday morning with a German disciple who is a world-renowned professor of physics. His deep understanding of physical science has only increased his amazement toward and faith in the Creator of it all. I learn from God's conversation with Job:

> "Can you bind the beautiful Pleiades?
>   Can you loose the cords of Orion?
> Can you bring forth the constellations in their seasons
>   or lead out the Bear with its cubs?
> Do you know the laws of the heavens?
>   Can you set up God's dominion over the earth?

> "Can you raise your voice to the clouds
>   and cover yourself with a flood of water?
> Do you send the lightning bolts on their way?
>   Do they report to you, 'Here we are'?" (Job 38:31–35)
>
> Then Job replied to the LORD:
>
> "I know that you can do all things;
>   no plan of yours can be thwarted.
> You asked, 'Who is this that obscures my counsel
>   without knowledge?'
> Surely I spoke of things I did not understand,
>   things too wonderful for me to know." (Job 42:1–3)

I take comfort in knowing that God has perfect global roaming. I count on this as I am traveling and have seen God answer specific prayers for the churches over here. Specifically, I have been praying that God would help bring about a revival in the youth and campus ministries. I am so amazed by God as I have heard of numerous teens getting baptized, and have heard how God provided some campus disciples to "just show up" here from other countries.

Yesterday I received two texts from my family informing me that in the same evening my oldest granddaughter had broken her arm, and my youngest grandson had been transported from the doctor's office to the hospital by ambulance because of a sudden, severe croup attack. It feels so helpless to be where I can't "do anything" but pray. Yet I realize that often prayer is the most important thing I can do! I count on the fact that although I am miles away, my prayers reach God and can touch the lives of my loved ones across the ocean. What a comfort! What an amazing God! The power of prayer is much more wonderful than global roaming.

> And pray in the Spirit on all occasions with all kinds of prayers and requests. With this in mind, be alert and always keep on praying for all the saints. (Ephesians 6:18)

Do not be anxious about anything, but in everything, by prayer and petition, with thanksgiving, present your requests to God. (Philippians 4:6)

Epaphras, who is one of you and a servant of Christ Jesus, sends greetings. He is always wrestling in prayer for you, that you may stand firm in all the will of God, mature and fully assured. (Colossians 4:12)

Pray continually. (1 Thessalonians 5:17)

For the eyes of the Lord are on the righteous
    and his ears are attentive to their prayer,
but the face of the Lord is against those who do evil.
(1 Peter 3:12)

The photo shows the German sky above me as I walked and prayed alongside a cornfield. Today when you look into the sky I hope you see more than just a blue expansive slate. Marvel at the great God who has ordered creation, and who can hear and act upon our prayers no matter where we are. Our prayers make more of a difference than we know.

caterpillar killer   20

I've been away from home this week. The day before we left, my friend Vanessa, who lives with us, pointed out a few small, yellow, worm-like caterpillars on the kitchen ceiling. Disgusted with their presence, and being a bit of a neat freak about keeping the kitchen clean and tidy, I climbed on top of the counter with a tissue and carefully smooshed the "things." A few days earlier, we had noticed some very small moths flying around the kitchen, so we surmised that these lovely worm things were related to the moths. The weather had been warmer than usual, so we figured it was just some kind of weird phenomenon that would last for the day. A few days ago (I was still out of the country), I received this Facebook message from Vanessa:

> Jeanie! The worms/maggots/larvae/whatever they are... took over the kitchen! I must've killed like 100 over the course of yesterday—it was so gross. But then it got worse. I started pulling food out of the pantry today to try to find out where they were coming from... and they were inside the cereal boxes and tons of other things! AHHHH! I was freaking out. I pulled out everything and found thousands

of the larvae on the very bottom of the pantry. I thought I was going to throw up... so gross. I'll probably have nightmares tonight. Anyway, I think I got it mostly cleaned up—we shall see. I keep feeling like I have worms crawling on me. I threw a lot of the cereal away (most of them were almost gone anyway) because they had gotten inside the boxes and then were hatching moths. Ugh. I could never be an exterminator!

My response: Oh no. I'm so sorry. Just got this message! That is absolutely disgusting! I wonder how this happens. I'd like to call them baby moth caterpillars. It sounds way better than maggots. I have to say, as gross as this is, your message makes me laugh just a little. Forgive me... Actually, I laughed out loud...

Vanessa: Hahaha. Well, I'm glad that it made you laugh! Just call me the Caterpillar Killer!

This disgusting turn of events made me wonder if I had consumed any of this "contaminated" cereal. This certainly gives new meaning to "butterflies in my stomach." It also reminded me of two scriptures. The first is Mark 7:20–23:

> He went on: "What comes out of a man is what makes him 'unclean.' For from within, out of men's hearts, come evil thoughts, sexual immorality, theft, murder, adultery, greed, malice, deceit, lewdness, envy, slander, arrogance and folly. All these evils come from inside and make a man 'unclean.'"

The second is Hebrews 12:15:

> See to it that no one misses the grace of God and that no bitter root grows up to cause trouble and defile many.

This little moth adventure is a reminder to me that unless I deal with the source of something bad, it will keep coming back!

Whacking the moths became a futile exercise. The sources—in the pantry, in the cereal boxes, and below—had to be completely removed! Will I (we) allow any bits of unforgiveness, greed, or deceit to dig into the corners of our hearts like the moth larvae did in the cereal boxes of my pantry? If so, the moths and the sins will keep coming. I want to pray as David did in Psalm 139:1–4, 23–24:

> O Lord, you have searched me
>   and you know me.
> You know when I sit and when I rise;
>   you perceive my thoughts from afar.
> You discern my going out and my lying down;
>   you are familiar with all my ways.
> Before a word is on my tongue
>   you know it completely, O Lord....
>
> Search me, O God, and know my heart;
>   test me and know my anxious thoughts.
> See if there is any offensive way in me,
>   and lead me in the way everlasting.

my solid rock 21

This was the view outside my bathroom window last week. I didn't get to enjoy it for long, as I had to cut short my trip. But I've held on to this picture in my mind, as the magnificence of this snow-covered mound of rock took my breath away. Ever since, I have often thought of this image along with several favorite scriptures about the "solid rock" that grounds me.

The LORD is my rock, my fortress and my deliverer;
   my God is my rock, in whom I take refuge.
   He is my shield and the horn of my salvation, my
      stronghold. (Psalm 18:2)

For in the day of trouble
   he will keep me safe in his dwelling;
he will hide me in the shelter of his tabernacle
   and set me high upon a rock. (Psalm 27:5)

From the ends of the earth I call to you,
   I call as my heart grows faint;
   lead me to the rock that is higher than I. (Psalm 61:2)

While I was away I kept receiving concerning texts. My granddaughter fell and broke her arm. The next day, my grandson was rushed from the doctor's office in an escorted ambulance to the hospital with an extremely severe case of croup. The following day, my pregnant daughter was taken from a doctor's visit to a large downtown hospital via ambulance, as she had begun active labor at thirty-two weeks. I found the next flight home, hoping I could make it before she delivered. I felt so helpless, but yet connected to the One who not only places me on this rock, but is also my refuge, deliverer, stronghold, and shelter. He is the One who is also able to move mountains. I cannot imagine going through life's trials without this solid rock. Without Christ, the solid rock, my life could be as described in the scripture below—slimy, muddy, and lost in the mire.

> He lifted me out of the slimy pit,
>   out of the mud and mire;
> he set my feet on a rock
>   and gave me a firm place to stand. (Psalm 40:2)

I made it back before delivery. The doctors were able to slow the progress and better prepare the lungs of our newest grandchild to be born: little Grace. At the time of this writing, labor was still slowly progressing, and my daughter was to be hospitalized until delivery. Micah's croup eventually went away, for which I was (and am) very grateful. I was grateful to be back home to help care for him while his mom was in the hospital and his dad was at work. Unfortunately, I ended up wrenching my back and dislocating three ribs, but thankfully, the chiropractor put them back in place.

What does all of this teach me? Trials will always come—sometimes all at once, it seems. I would have liked to avoid all these trials, but my God gives me a firm place on which to stand. Sometimes I feel like I slip and lose my footing, but then he grounds me again. I'm so grateful for my solid rock.

getting rid of "rotten apple" 22

Sometimes life moves at a challenging pace. The past several weeks have been particularly swift and difficult. Amidst all of our family drama over the past few weeks (much of which I have written about in the previous chapters), a week ago our church hosted a large national conference, which kept us all very busy. The conference also included some pre-meetings and post-meetings for me... all good, but tiring nonetheless. By the last day of the conference, I felt a level of tiredness than made it difficult for me to function with a sense of alertness. Throughout the conference, I had been shuttling my youngest grandson back and forth to a downtown hospital to see his mother—my daughter Kristen. She is still "holding" in preterm labor as I write. She's been hospitalized for sixteen days now, and for many of those days I've had the wonderful privilege of keeping her twenty-month-old son. He's been wonderful, even though it's been a confusing time for him.

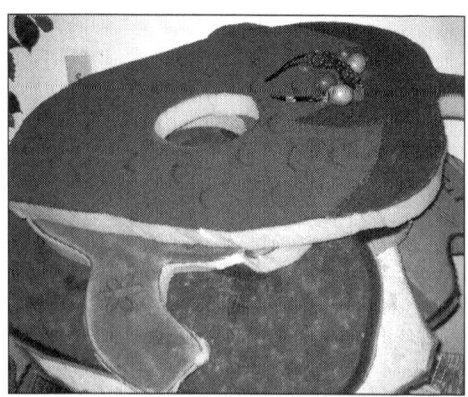

The last day of the conference, I awoke with a terrible cold, and stared with dismay at the bag in my hotel room containing a fruit-patterned apron, a headband draped with plastic fruit, and a pile of large foam fruit heads. I wasn't ready to face the task this bag represented, and I needed help to get my heart into what was to come that morning: an action-packed, song- and dance-filled hour of "Fruity Tunes." I was supposed to perform for about two hundred children as the character Fruity Tunes (the main character in my book for children, *Fruity Tunes and the Adventures of Rotten Apple*).

I prayed that morning to claim the promise in Colossians 1:29—of the energy that God promises he can mightily inspire within me.

> For this I toil and struggle with all the energy that he powerfully inspires within me. (Colossians 1:29, NRSV)

I'll share a short synopsis of the simple message of *Fruity Tunes*: My character, Fruity, introduces Loving Lemon, Smiley Strawberry, Peaceful Pineapple, and Patient Peach to all the children. These "spiritual fruits" all have messages and songs for the children. After each introduction, performed through songs and dance, Rotten Apple appears, bringing his terrible messages and dreadful songs. He threatens to take away the love, joy, peace, and patience that are being offered by the fruits. Fruity helps the children chase Rotten Apple away with scriptures and songs. Tippety Teapot gets involved in the action as she helps the children continually pour out their love, joy, peace, and patience. In the end, the fruits and teapot unite the children in pouring out all of God's love, joy, peace, and patience onto Rotten Apple. This turns him into a happy, loving, sweet, and repentant apple!

This simple message was just what I needed that morning. Before we started, I really didn't feel like giving, loving, or being joyfully excited or animated. Satan, whether by circumstances, ill health, or various temptations, is always trying to steal our love, joy, peace, and patience. But God, through his Spirit, continually pours these qualities into our hearts. I'm so grateful for this promise!

> Not only so, but we also rejoice in our sufferings, because we know that suffering produces perseverance; perseverance, character; and character, hope. And hope does

not disappoint us, because **God has poured out his love into our hearts by the Holy Spirit, whom he has given us.** (Romans 5:3–5, emphasis added)

Fruity calls for the children to read a Bible verse and to sing a song in order to send Rotten Apple away. Funny... I find the same things help me!

the particularly persistent purple petunia   23

In my first devotional book, *My Morning Cup,* I wrote about a particularly persistent purple petunia. In the chapter entitled "When I Sit in the Backyard" I wrote:

> One of my favorite backyard stories teaches me perseverance. One cold February day after the snow had partially melted, I saw something purple on the ground. Upon closer scrutiny, I discovered it was a pansy peeking through the snow. [I have since learned that it was a petunia.] I had planted it the previous summer, and it should not have survived the harsh winter. It was not meant to be that hardy. However, it survived, and it thrived. I took a photo to remind me of the lessons I wanted to remember from that fragile but tough "pansy" (that sounds like an oxymoron). With God, we have the opportunity to keep blooming when the circumstances are tough. Paul describes this kind of faith in 2 Corinthians 4:9 when he says, "We may be knocked down but never knocked out" (J.B. Phillips translation).

A few days ago, I was greatly encouraged by a new sighting of a purple petunia! My time and attention had been "extra occupied" and I'd had little time for extended prayer, study, writing, or thinking. I felt as though I was going from one thing to the next, and felt a little more spent than usual. I had not taken much time to process the things going on around me in my mind and heart, and I needed some rest.

Then I thought about my daughter. She would love to be up

 and busy, but she was completing a month of hospitalized bed rest. Both of these challenges—being very busy, and being forced to be still—take perseverance. As with most things that require waiting, repetition, and "keeping on keeping on," we don't always see an immediate end, reward, or response. As I walked out my front door and saw this new lone purple petunia, this scripture came to mind:

> Do not be deceived: God cannot be mocked. A man reaps what he sows. The one who sows to please his sinful nature, from that nature will reap destruction; the one who sows to please the Spirit, from the Spirit will reap eternal life. **Let us not become weary in doing good, for at the proper time we will reap a harvest if we do not give up.** Therefore, as we have opportunity, let us do good to all people, especially to those who belong to the family of believers. (Galatians 6:7–10, emphasis added)

That same petunia was alive and well, yet again. It was not in the exact same place, and didn't look exactly the same, but it was back again! This beautiful purple flower that had come from the one planted several years before had found a way to bloom again—it was not even the season for petunias to be blooming. The original plant was long gone. Yet this lone bloom appeared on my landing, about fifteen feet away from where the original one once grew.

This flower has taught me about life yet again. Some of the good things we do as a matter of routine, day after day, may not reap a harvest until later. Whatever you may be weary of doing, take heart and keep on going! You never know when and where the resulting harvest will appear.

As you do not know the path of the wind,
> or how the body is formed in a mother's womb,
so you cannot understand the work of God,
> the Maker of all things.

Sow your seed in the morning,
> and at evening let not your hands be idle,
for you do not know which will succeed,
> whether this or that,
> or whether both will do equally well.

(Ecclesiastes 11:5–6)

our little mirrors   24

I had the privilege for several weeks to spend some extra time with several of my grandchildren. Kristen's prescribed bed rest gave me extra opportunities to take little Micah along as my assistant during some days. Also, Melissa and Kevin were traveling, and so I watched their three children on a Sunday afternoon and evening. I was amazed as I watched—and was reminded how much children absorb the things they see and hear around them. They take in the words, faith, attitudes, purposes, and values they see portrayed. They listen to and imitate what they see with incredible perception and accuracy. I am particularly reminded of two scriptures that teach this axiom.

> "A student is not above his teacher, but everyone who is fully trained will be like his teacher." (Luke 6:40)

> Finally, brothers, whatever is true, whatever is noble, whatever is right, whatever is pure, whatever is lovely, whatever is admirable—if anything is excellent or praiseworthy—think about such things. Whatever you have learned or received or heard from me, or seen in me—put it into practice. And the God of peace will be with you. (Philippians 4:8–9)

We learn best from what we see modeled and communicated from one heart to another. I love watching my grown children parent their children. I am so proud of them and the ways they are training their children. Earlier this week I received this picture from Melissa, with the following text:

Lexi to me with my shoes and book: "Bye Mom. I'm going to a Bible study. I gotta preach 'bout Jesus."

Lexi was imitating what she saw in her mom and dad. This reminded me how much our lives are like mirrors—always. I am grateful that I can continue to learn from the mirror of the Scriptures as well as from watching others who have strengths I wish to emulate. We diligently strove to put the following scripture into practice when our children were young:

> Hear, O Israel: The LORD our God, the LORD is one. Love the LORD your God with all your heart and with all your soul and with all your strength. These commandments that I give you today are to be upon your hearts. Impress them on your children. Talk about them when you sit at home and when you walk along the road, when you lie down and when you get up. (Deuteronomy 6:4–7)

My parents did this as well. Of all the things I remember about my parents, the thing that stands out the most is that they loved God with all their heart, soul, and strength. Whatever is "first" in our life is clear to our children. Our words, actions, compassion, faith, attitudes, and purposes will shine through... one way or another.

Today, and each day, may we be alert to learning and teaching ways that are pleasing to God.

from the sewer   25

We have had a large storm and have lost power. As I am going on my fourth day without electricity, I am reminded of the millions of children (and their parents) who daily go to bed hungry, cold, and without running water. I have been given so much, and I need to remind my heart to be generous and gracious—and to more closely strive to follow in Jesus' steps. I am reminded of people I have seen firsthand around the world...

During the eight years when I was employed by the wonderful benevolent organization HOPE Worldwide, I did quite a bit of traveling. Our children were still in school at the time and our extended families lived far away, so I had to be confident that the value of my travel outweighed the difficulties of being away from my children. While I was able to see amazing parts of God's handiwork across the globe, my travel with HOPE was not to the typical vacation sites. Instead, I had the privilege of visiting many of the world's most severe slums.

When I encountered children in their difficult surroundings, sometimes I felt my tears would not stop flowing. I had the opportunity to visit with children roaming the streets, and lepers whose limbs had been eaten away. I saw children who were organized by pimps for sex trade, and visited children with AIDS who were dying alone. I saw young boys with bags of paint pressed to their noses in order to get high as they traveled the subway alleys. I talked and played with hundreds of children who had no parents. I enjoyed the company of some young ones who lived on top of garbage heaps, and others who were hungry.

My memories are vivid of one particular day when I climbed

down into the sewers of Romania. I encountered not only children, but also teenagers who had children of their own. I took a snapshot of one little family. Their one request was that I come back with the printed picture of them, as they had never owned a photo. Like a broken record, over and over I heard the words, "Can you help me?" I felt so helpless in comparison to the magnitude of the needs.

Even now, as I think about these individual souls, I can feel overwhelmed with the task of responding to their pleas for help. As we walked the sewer passages, we had flashlights and candles to light the way and to allow us to see people's faces. While in the sewer I learned many lessons. I pray I never forget them.

I can't do everything, but I can do what I can. I am reminded of the woman Jesus commended in Mark 14:3–9:

> While he was in Bethany, reclining at the table in the home of a man known as Simon the Leper, a woman came with an alabaster jar of very expensive perfume, made of pure nard. She broke the jar and poured the perfume on his head.
> Some of those present were saying indignantly to one another, "Why this waste of perfume? It could have been sold for more than a year's wages and the money given to the poor." And they rebuked her harshly.
> "Leave her alone," said Jesus. "Why are you bothering

her? She has done a beautiful thing to me. The poor you will always have with you, and you can help them any time you want. But you will not always have me. She did what she could. She poured perfume on my body beforehand to prepare for my burial. I tell you the truth, wherever the gospel is preached throughout the world, what she has done will also be told, in memory of her."

Even in this account, Jesus knows that the plight of the poor will always be with us.

I have realized that I need those who are poor in my life. They awaken my compassion, but also test and "grow" my heart. They help me know whether my Christianity is theoretical or real. In this passage Jesus visits the home of a leper. We then see a woman come to anoint Jesus, which he describes as an act preparing him for burial. That appreciation and pure, devoted love for Jesus is held up as an example for me and for all of us. I need to consistently help the poor, but also keep my devotion to the Lord as first importance.

When I remember walking through that sewer, I find insight from Job as he seeks to understand and defend his plight. His words are a continual upward call to me.

> "Whoever heard me spoke well of me,
>   and those who saw me commended me,
> because I rescued the poor who cried for help,
>   and the fatherless who had none to assist him.
> The man who was dying blessed me;
>   I made the widow's heart sing.
> I put on righteousness as my clothing;
>   justice was my robe and my turban.
> I was eyes to the blind
>   and feet to the lame.
> I was a father to the needy;
>   I took up the case of the stranger.
> I broke the fangs of the wicked
>   and snatched the victims from their teeth."
> (Job 29:11–17)

I know I have a long way to go to have this kind of heart and reputation. The sewer reminds me of the need, but I live a long way from that sewer. However, wherever I go I can speak up, and I can have an open hand.

> Speak up for those who cannot speak for themselves,
>   for the rights of all who are destitute. (Proverbs 31:8)

> There will always be poor people in the land. Therefore I command you to be openhanded toward your brothers and toward the poor and needy in your land.
> (Deuteronomy 15:11)

May we remember the poor as we remember the words of Jesus in Matthew 5:16:

> "In the same way, let your light shine before men, that they may see your good deeds and praise your Father in heaven."

old dog syndrome   26

After a spring snowstorm, our electricity went out, so the dogs and I went to stay with my daughter and her family. The next morning I drove to my house to clean out my freezer. While I was there, our power returned, so I went back to my daughter's house to collect the dogs and return home.

Jordan, our fourteen-year-old golden retriever, was lying on the floor when I arrived. My daughter told me he was not able get up. He looked disoriented and scared, and seemed to be in a bad way. I called the vet, who was eager to see him. When my son-in-law returned from work, he loaded Jordan into my car so I could take him to his appointment. Fearing the worst, I cried all the way to the vet's office, praying and telling God that I needed my husband for this scary ordeal. Wyndham was on a plane, due to arrive home later in the night.

When I arrived at the vet, I began to sob, thinking of all the wonderful memories with Jordan, and fearing that I might not ever take him home again. I felt sad that my husband might not be able to tell his beloved dog good-bye. Our doctor (who is very partial to golden retrievers) carried him in for an examination and explained that he had "Old Dog Vestibular Syndrome." The great news was that in eighty-five percent of cases it clears up within a week.

Happily, I brought Jordan back home and my neighbor carried him inside for me. I was told that he would be an invalid during this time and would need extra TLC and reassurance, as the illness was frightening to him as well. Jordan would have to be carried outside (and he weighs more than sixty pounds).

Wyndham arrived back late that night. He carried the dog

out and repeated the process the next morning, hoping Jordan would figure a way to relieve himself (which he did, though I will spare you details). This syndrome causes a dog's head to tilt and their eyes to twitch. The dogs are often nauseated because they lose all sense of balance—they don't know which way is up or which way is down. Watching Jordan try to walk was pitiful. He looked like an old man in a drunken stupor, walking in wobbly circles before falling down.

As I heard him whimpering before daylight one morning, I went out to lie on the floor beside him (a mother's ears are always tuned in to pain). I realized that I was likely rather pathetic looking—lying on the floor beside our dog while our other dog was stretched out on the sofa above me. However, immediately after I lay down beside him, Jordan fell asleep. Since the floor was hard, I did more thinking than sleeping. I thought  about how Jesus felt about those around him who were completely disoriented by their own choices and their refusal to look to him for direction.

> When Jesus landed and saw a large crowd, he had compassion on them, because they were like sheep without a shepherd. So he began teaching them many things. (Mark 6:34)

I also thought of Galatians 6:2:

> Carry each other's burdens, and in this way you will fulfill the law of Christ.

I pray that watching Jordan's helplessness will help me to see others more closely through Jesus' eyes of compassion. As much as I love Jordan, I know each person is so much more a treasure—however disoriented, helpless, and harassed they may be.

almost taken out by the trash truck   27

"Stop! Stop!" I screamed. I went tearing out of my house in my bathrobe across the snowy grass to the middle of the road. Our dog Jordan was stretched out on the road and a huge garbage truck was barreling toward him at full speed.

As I wrote in the previous chapter, Jordan had a temporary illness called Old Dog Vestibular Syndrome, which is supposed to last about a week. He was completely disoriented and nauseated, and he couldn't walk without trembling and falling over. This particular morning, Wyndham had lovingly carried Jordan outside for his morning business, and then let him lie in the grass to enjoy the outdoor sun while Wyndham ventured out for a prayer walk. Watching his master walk off without him was more

than Jordan could bear. He somehow found a way to get up, and he tried to follow Wyndham. He only made it to the middle of the street, where he lay helpless. I looked out of the window just in time to see this near-tragedy unfolding.

As I raced across the lawn, I watched the truck speeding down the road—and then I couldn't see Jordan anymore. My heart sank. Then, as the truck passed, I saw Jordan's sad eyes looking up at me. The truck had missed him by inches. I ran over and snatched him up into my arms, all sixty-plus pounds of him (adrenaline works well in these situations), and carried him back inside. My heart was still pounding, but I was grateful for the good outcome, and that Wyndham would not face a devastating situation upon his return.

I realize I may have lost those of you who are not "dog people," but many of you can relate to my feelings. As I took some time that morning to "be still and know that he is God" (from Psalm 46:10), I thought about this situation and the lessons I could learn from it.

Immediately, one of my favorite scriptures in Jude came to mind:

> But you, dear friends, build yourselves up in your most holy faith and pray in the Holy Spirit. Keep yourselves in God's love as you wait for the mercy of our Lord Jesus Christ to bring you to eternal life.
> Be merciful to those who doubt; snatch others from the fire and save them; to others show mercy, mixed with fear—hating even the clothing stained by corrupted flesh. To him who is able to keep you from falling and to present you before his glorious presence without fault and with great joy—to the only God our Savior be glory, majesty, power and authority, through Jesus Christ our Lord, before all ages, now and forevermore! Amen. (vv. 20–25)

What an upward call to me today in the following ways:

- to take personal responsibility to build myself up in holy faith and to pray.
- to keep myself in God's love... and not spiritually wander, making myself more vulnerable to "garbage" running over me.
- to be merciful to those who doubt.
- to have as much concern for my spiritual family as I felt this morning for Jordan; to never forget the need to snatch people from harm's way.

I'm inspired by Jude's benediction reminding me that my God is able to keep me from falling, and to present me to himself, through Jesus, without fault and with great joy. Wow.

carried close to his heart   28

> He tends his flock like a shepherd:
>   He gathers the lambs in his arms
> and carries them close to his heart;
>   he gently leads those that have young. (Isaiah 40:11)

I think of this verse each time I watch my husband carry Jordan in and out of the house first thing in the morning and last thing at night. This new routine is causing Wyndham some back soreness, but we think it's worth it. This caretaking responsibility is teaching me many lessons, but is very sad.

Saturday morning I had a good cry—actually a deep sob is more accurate. Jordan had not eaten or had water in two days. He could not stand. Wyndham and I concurred that we would wait two or three days to decide whether or not to put him down. I felt the inevitable was approaching.

I made Jordan scrambled eggs, meat, and chicken soup, and offered them all to him. He had no interest. Then he surprised me. Saturday night, on a whim, I tried feeding him Ritz crackers with peanut butter on them. Apparently, that hit the spot. He ate the whole roll of crackers. Yesterday he had about four hamburgers, a chocolate chip cookie (his favorite—and chocolate has never hurt him in all his fourteen years), and he drank a lot of water. Last night he stood up. This morning I cooked some ground beef (with some mashed sweet potatoes added) and he ate it all from my hand. Then after we carried him outside, he stood up, did his business, and wagged his tail. It seems he truly is getting better! Whether or not he will fully recover is still unknown, but I'm encouraged.

Meanwhile, I think about the fact that he is our dog—a perfectly wonderful dog, mind you—but I do realize he is not (quite) human. I think about the tender loving care he needs right now and how eager I am to give it. And I am a very imperfect human.

I can't really begin to grasp the love God extends to me. It floors me to think that I am made in his image, thought of even before I was born (Psalm 139), and that he gathers me in his arms—close to his heart, as Isaiah 40 says. Shamefully, I worry about too many things. The next time I am tempted to worry about something (likely later tonight), I need to remember how I feel about my dog, and then remember God's loving care for me, his sheep. Nothing is too big (or too little) for my God.

> Then Jesus said to his disciples: "Therefore I tell you, do not worry about your life, what you will eat; or about your body, what you will wear. Life is more than food, and the body more than clothes. Consider the ravens: They do not sow or reap, they have no storeroom or barn; yet God feeds them. And how much more valuable you are than birds! Who of you by worrying can add a single hour to his life? Since you cannot do this very little thing, why do you worry about the rest?" (Luke 12:22–26)

a listening ear 29

My ears seem too sensitized lately, and it's affecting my sleep. For the past six weeks I have had my phone in my room at night—on standby for baby delivery news. For three of those weeks, while Kristen was hospitalized, my ears were also tuned in to the baby monitor in our room in case my grandson awoke upstairs. I found I would wake up to the slightest stirring. I even started incorporating the ring of a phone or the croupy cough of my grandson into my dreams. Sometimes I would wake up only to realize that I was just hearing my own breathing.

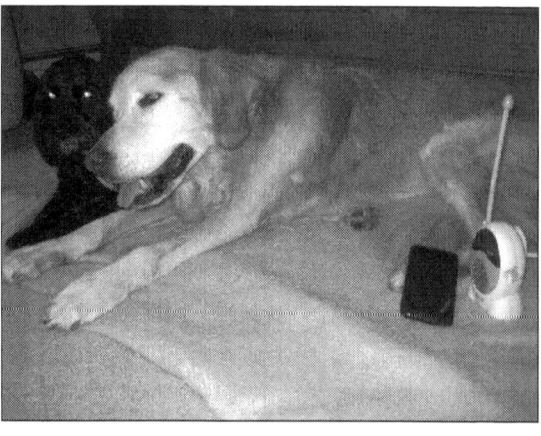

Now, I also hear whimpering through the night from Jordan, our ailing golden retriever. He used to be so quiet. Now he is excited when he stands up, and he wants to let us know. He barks when he needs to go out, when he wants water, and when he wants another PBJ (peanut butter and jelly sandwich, his new favorite). He still doesn't want his dog food (hmmm, I wonder why). Last night he began barking for no apparent reason. It seems he was lonely. Once we brought him into our room he was fine. He just wanted company.

Tonight I was tempted to put my noise-canceling earphones on and just fall asleep listening to Kenny G... or better yet, listening to quietness. However, I need to be able to hear since I'm "on call."

I started thinking about how amazing God is. He is always on call.

> Evening, morning and noon
>   I cry out in distress,
>   and he hears my voice. (Psalm 55:17)

He never sleeps (Psalm 121:3–4). His ears are always attentive to the cries of the righteous.

> For the eyes of the Lord are on the righteous
>   and his ears are attentive to their prayer,
> but the face of the Lord is against those who do evil.
> (1 Peter 3:12)

This blows my mind. This is a dimension beyond my understanding. I can tire by just being attentive to my immediate family (dogs included). God is listening for all those who are seeking him, and attentive to all those who are striving to follow him.

It is also a sobering thought to realize that God does not hear when we aren't seeking him or trying to follow him.

> But your iniquities have separated
>   you from your God;
> your sins have hidden his face from you,
>   so that he will not hear. (Isaiah 59:2)

I'm so grateful that God wants to hear my voice.

> In the morning, O Lord, you hear my voice;
>   in the morning I lay my requests before you
>   and wait in expectation. (Psalm 5:3)

I want to be most sensitized to hearing God. I want to hear him as I read my Bible, as I ask for wisdom, and as I try to be tuned in to his Spirit. I pray that today I can be "on call" to his voice.

> "My sheep listen to my voice; I know them, and they follow me." (John 10:27)

good-bye ol' friend 30
(Jordan Shaw, July 3, 1997–November 15, 2011)

I can't say I've ever written a letter to a dog before. However, as I say good-bye to you, my furry friend, I want to thank you for several things. I think you know them, but it's therapeutic for me to write them.

It seems a mere "blink" ago when Wyndham and I decided, while on a marriage getaway, to look for you. We found you in Maine and stopped by camp to surprise the kids with you on our way home. They were so thrilled they could hardly contain themselves. I felt an instant kinship with you, Jordan, as we got carsick together on the way home. Proverbs 6:6 tells of what we can learn from watching the ways of an ant. Let  me tell you ten things I have learned from watching you—the ways of an amazing golden retriever.

1. You stretched yourself: You were pretty fast yourself, but when you were youngster, I loved watching you run with Pharaoh, the neighborhood greyhound. You tried so hard to keep up, and made yourself stronger and faster by having a buddy like that. I, too, always need to surround myself with people who are better at things than I am. It makes me grow.

2. You thrilled at your purpose: You came from a hunting heritage. It was a beautiful thing to see you hunt pheasant (as I've seen from the videos). You gave your master, Wyndham, so many great memories. Your instinct was natural. God made you to hunt birds, and you did it well. Though perhaps a "spoiled bird dog," you loved the thrill of finding birds. (Well… except the one extremely cold, rainy morning when you knew Wyndham was going hunting and you hid under the covers at my feet. He looked all over for you. I told you I wouldn't tell… but finally had to "spill the beans"—sorry. However, I heard you did enjoy it after all.) When you started to get too old to hunt, you went out with the new little guys (the goldens we got for Sam and Kristen) and showed them what to do. You trained them when you got too old to run. Likewise, I know I am so much happier when I am living out the purpose for which God created me. And as I age I want to be all about passing what I have learned on to others.
3. You made friends with everyone: I called you the "mayor of the park." Since we live across the street from a park, you assumed every person or dog that came was there to be your friend. So many people in this town know your name. You loved everyone. You joined in a few soccer games, ended up at neighbors' homes, and even had little girls down the street come knock on our door every afternoon after school to ask, "Can Jordan come out to play with us?" You have introduced me to so many people, and remembering your ways encourages me to try to make friends with new people.
4. You loved children: You were the best dog a kid or grown-up could have. You made Jacob's transition into our home so much easier for him… as you seemed to understand Romanian better than anyone. He had many conversations with you. You raced our kids down many a hill while they

were sledding. You welcomed each of the grandchildren—and even let them ride you like a horse. Even in these last few days, feeling so badly, you patiently lay still while Micah held you around your torso to hug you and kiss you.
5. You cared, in your own doggy way: You had a keen sensitivity to emotions. Whenever I was sad you would just come close to be near. That's all. Whenever anyone came over to talk with us... if they were hurting or crying you always chose to sit close to them. Somehow you knew. I see how sometimes just being there really helps.
6. You took care of your "little brother" and endured his neediness of you: Poor Blackie (our cockerpoo, named by Jacob, who received him as a Christmas gift ten years ago) will be lost for a while without you. He has never known life away from you. He slept inside of your four legs, all scooched up to your stomach. Thinking he is part cat, he constantly groomed you, from the insides of your ears to your gums (I know... disgusting)—and you let him! Even last week, though you couldn't walk, you somehow managed to get up when he was being chased by a dog. You were a great big brother. I can sometimes get annoyed by others' neediness. May I learn to have the patience you showed.
7. You weren't afraid to ask: You loved sweets, particularly chocolate chip cookies. I never could resist those eyes. They caused me to give my food away to you, even the last licks of my ice cream (and I don't like to part with my ice cream). You assumed I should have a piece of popcorn and then you should get a piece... and back and forth we would go. You mastered the art of propping your head on my knee and giving me the "sad eyes." You loved our "Nana and Papa nights" where you got lots of pizza from begging with all the grandkids. You were persistent, and

it worked. While I don't want to be a nag, sometimes I lack the courage to ask for things.

8. You never had a bad day: You were so consistent in your demeanor—always happy. You got Lyme disease several times, were hit by a car once, got skunked a few times, and were constantly losing your hair. (Wow, I even think I'll miss using the lint roller several times a day.) You were in pain often this last year, but never complained. You just stayed happy. This is one more reason it's just hard to say good-bye. May I be as content as you were.

9. You grew old with dignity: These last few days you tried so hard to help us out when it came time to carry you outside. I know you wanted to do for yourself, and it was hard on you to be so needy. When you could still walk, you would sometimes need an encouraging word to go up the stairs, but you would push yourself hard. I think you would truly rather die than "mess up" in the house. You liked privacy when you did your business. You remind me that, even though you were a dog, you had dignity about you. How much more do I need to honor those who are aging and show them dignity and respect?

10. You lived to please your master: This is what stands out to me the most, old friend. You truly did live to please your master. Nothing pleased you more than to please first Wyndham, and then me. As I write this with tears stream-  ing, I pray that what can most be said about my life is that I lived to please my master. Nothing better could be said.

good-bye ol' friend

Thank you for fourteen golden years, golden boy. I will miss you more than you could ever know.

There is a time for everything,
and a season for every activity under heaven:
a time to be born and a time to die,
a time to plant and a time to uproot,
a time to kill and a time to heal,
a time to tear down and a time to build,
a time to weep and a time to laugh,
a time to mourn and a time to dance,
a time to scatter stones and a time to gather them,
a time to embrace and a time to refrain,
a time to search and a time to give up,
a time to keep and a time to throw away,
a time to tear and a time to mend,
a time to be silent and a time to speak,
a time to love and a time to hate,
a time for war and a time for peace.
(Ecclesiastes 3:1–8)

the circle of life 31

The circle keeps on turning. Over the past two months I've keenly felt its spin. After burying Wyndham's dad in early fall, I reflected how short a long life of ninety-two years really is in the scheme of time. The scripture is so true in James 4:14:

> Why, you do not even know what will happen tomorrow. What is your life? You are a mist that appears for a little while and then vanishes.

A week ago I witnessed the dramatic birth of my newest grandchild, who is aptly named Grace. Although she tried mightily to make her debut much too early, God graciously answered yes to our pleas for her to stay put long enough to be healthy. I shared earlier the scripture from Jeremiah 29:11–13 that emboldened my spirit as I watched this new life emerge:

> "For I know the plans I have for you," declares the LORD, "plans to prosper you and not to harm you, plans to give you hope and a future. Then you will call upon me and come and pray to me, and I will listen to you. You will seek me and find me when you seek me with all your heart."

the circle of life

A few days ago my firstborn turned thirty-four... hard to believe. In many ways it seems like yesterday when I was thirty-four, and yet in other ways it seems like eons ago. So much life has been lived, and I look forward to the gift of each new day God gives me. Every day truly is a gift from God.

> This is the day the LORD has made;
> let us rejoice and be glad in it. (Psalm 118:24)

Last week we lost our dog, who was such a part of our family. At fourteen and a half, he had already outlived his life expectancy. The circle of life keeps on spinning. Sometimes it exhilarates my heart, and at other times it seems to break it into pieces.

When I keep the perspective that each day is a gift from God, full of opportunity to live out his purpose for my life, it affords a *joie de vivre* that makes a huge difference in my own quality of life, as well as in the impact I can have on those whose lives I touch. I was moved by my Bible reading today as I read of David in Acts 13:22.

> "After removing Saul, he made David their king. He testified concerning him: 'I have found David son of Jesse a man after my own heart; he will do everything I want him to do.'"

What a tribute! Here a man, though flawed, is recorded for all history as a man after God's own heart—doing everything God has planned for him. I then read on to verse 36:

> "For when David had served God's purpose in his own generation, he fell asleep; he was buried with his fathers and his body decayed. But the one whom God raised from the dead did not see decay."

What a profound statement about his life—he "served God's purpose in his own generation." It is simple, yet profound. We certainly are not just bodies with souls inside. We are souls created for a purpose that happen to be surrounded by temporary bodies. When we are born spiritually, these souls will live forever.

> Now that you have purified yourselves by obeying the truth so that you have sincere love for your brothers, love one another deeply, from the heart. For you have been born again, not of perishable seed, but of imperishable, through the living and enduring word of God. For,
>
> "All men are like grass,
>   and all their glory is like the flowers of the field;
> the grass withers and the flowers fall,
>   but the word of the Lord stands forever."
> (1 Peter 1:22–25)

I pray to be about God's purpose in my life today and each day. I'm grateful that his word clarifies that purpose for me. It is sometimes thrilling, sometimes scary, sometimes difficult—but it is always so right and so good when God stays at the center of this spinning circle.

show me 32

I'm a visual learner. You can tell me something, and I may or may not remember or understand it. For instance, as a young teen I volunteered in a hospital as a candy striper. I thought I might want to enter the medical profession one day, so I wanted to get some hands-on experience. On my first day of candy striping, I was given an assignment (not a particularly technical one!) to fill all the water pitchers with ice for the patients in a particular wing of the hospital. I don't know why, but I remember that almost all of the patients were men. I was busy about my task and had nearly finished, when one of the men chuckled, looked at me, and said, "This gives new meaning to 'peeing on the rocks.'"

I had filled up all of the urinals with ice water! I decided that day that the medical profession was not for me. I had certainly missed something between instruction and implementation. I obviously needed someone to show me what to do.

I recently returned from a conference in Budapest, Hungary. As I travel, I am often struck by how much clearer life seems from the view thirty-five thousand feet above the earth. Looking down from a plane, everything looks so neat, orderly, and simple. Yet I know that in reality, confusion, bitterness, and loneliness reign within most individuals down below. While God's word is very clear, I am moved to know that God's heart was grieved when he looked down and saw evil and the resulting pain in the world.

> The LORD was grieved that he had made man on the earth, and his heart was filled with pain. (Genesis 6:6)

I am so grateful that I have a compassionate God who came down here to show me how to live. As he continually intervened in hearts and lives, working through people and circumstances, I wonder what conversations may have gone on between God and his Son. I wonder what was said as they prepared for Jesus to come down and show us how to live. I am so thankful that God didn't look down with mere disgust and anger (which he certainly could have), but instead looked with such love that he sent his beloved Son to show us the way we were created to live. He would not only show us how to live, but would also enable us to break free from the power of sin and the resulting separation from our Father.

> They were all filled with awe and praised God. "A great prophet has appeared among us," they said. "God has come to help his people." (Luke 7:16)

God had already communicated clearly, but he went beyond words. He came to help. He showed us how.

> The Word became flesh and made his dwelling among us. We have seen his glory, the glory of the One and Only, who came from the Father, full of grace and truth. (John 1:14)

He didn't have to—but he cared so much that he did. Thank you, Jesus, for showing me how to love, how to forgive, how to relate to others, how to communicate, how to have purpose, and how to think.

> This is how God showed his love among us: He sent his one and only Son into the world that we might live through him. (1 John 4:9)

If I didn't have Jesus showing me how to live real life every day, I would be lost—and running around "filling urinals" while people around me were thirsting for water.

snippets of love 33

Our Christmas cards almost didn't go out this year due to a condition I call "communication stuckness." This is a condition that sometimes affects me. It can happen when there is so much to say, or so many  things to catch up on, that I don't know where to start. Unfortunately, the result can mean that I get stuck.

My husband tells me my brain seldom rests. I'm always thinking about something, which can lead to information overload. Then, my communication can get out of sync with what goes on in my head, ultimately leading to "communication stuckness."

For example, when my mom was still living, I made it a goal to write her weekly. At first I used "snail mail," but later we communicated by email. Since she was deaf for many years, she relied on written communication. I thought about writing her nearly every day, but too often I would get stuck when actually trying to follow through on that intention. Often it seemed there was so much to say that I would not know where to start—so I ended up writing less often than I wished. My sister suggested that instead of trying to write *more* things *less* often, I should try writing *less* things *more* often—perhaps a few sentences several times a week. She suggested that I could even forward my mom an interesting or humorous article that I'd received. It was important that I communicated frequently enough to let her know how often I lovingly thought of her.

At times I can find the same challenge of "overload stuckness" in my communication with God. I think about him throughout the day and communicate often in my head (and heart). However, I can get stuck when I feel there is so much to pray about that I can't even remember it all—and feel it would take hours just to mention everything I need and want to pray about. I know that communication with God in prayer and in listening to him through the Scriptures is the most important part of my life, so I want to overcome the communication block that sometimes occurs.

I am grateful for the instruction and challenges in the Scriptures that encourage me in these things.

In 1 Thessalonians 5:16–18, Paul states:

> Be joyful always; pray continually; give thanks in all circumstances, for this is God's will for you in Christ Jesus.

I learn from this that throughout the day I can give "love snippets" of gratitude: short expressions of love to God throughout the day. He wants to know I am thinking of him.

I also realize that communication takes preparation, watchfulness, and devotion. It takes hard work and discipline, as described by the term "wrestling" in the scripture below:

> Devote yourselves to prayer, being watchful and thankful. (Colossians 4:2)

> Epaphras, who is one of you and a servant of Christ Jesus, sends greetings. He is always wrestling in prayer for you, that you may stand firm in all the will of God, mature and fully assured. (Colossians 4:12)

I'm going forward with a plan designed to help me overcome "communication stuckness" so that I can be more devoted, watchful, and thankful in my prayers. I crafted a little organizational tool to help me with this. It's a simple laminated bookmark with an "assigned by me" topic for prayer focus each day. When there is a lot of information to pray about and act upon, I get lost and stuck without organization. I've found it helpful to have specific days focused on specific things. I plan to use this to accompany the snippets of communication throughout the day.

I desire to also become more effective in communicating my appreciation to others more often by using shorter snippets instead of getting stuck in overload. I have even decided that it is okay to sign my Christmas cards with the simple note, "Love, the Shaws."

If I tried to write more, I might still be stuck, pen in hand, with a pile of envelopes by my side.

out of gas   34

Funny how empty the house can seem after Christmas. The last of our family members has just pulled out of the driveway, and our house is suddenly quiet. No more squeals, pitter-patter of little feet, giggles, or shouts of, "Mom! She's trying to get my stuff!" fill the air. I miss that "music." I'm so grateful that my children and grandchildren live close by, but there is still something a little sad about the day after Christmas. Part of the reason for the sadness, I think, is that I'm exhausted.

I love Christmastime and all the music, baking, cooking, decorating, and wrapping that go with it. Most of the time I love it... but sometimes I'm just tired. Today, after some cleaning up, to be honest, I felt like I was all out of the "giving spirit." I began reading and catching up on recent online events, including news about a tragic fire in New England that killed a woman's three children and her parents early Christmas morning. I then felt very sad all afternoon. This made me feel even less like giving. Frankly, I felt like I was out of gas.

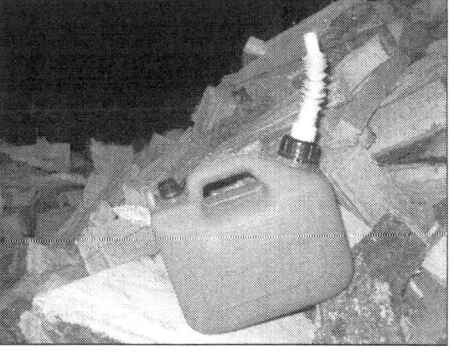

Have you ever been driving and run out of gas? I have. I remember a particular episode years ago (in our pre-children days) when our dog ran away. I had let him out before I went to bed, but he didn't return for the entire night. I couldn't sleep from worrying about our little cocker spaniel. As we searched the neighborhood the next day, I discovered that a neighbor living about a half mile away also had a dog that was missing. It was an Afghan hound who happened to be "in heat." I put two and two together and figured that we would likely find my male dog hanging out with her female dog. I called the local animal shelter ("local" in that it was in the state—it was about thirty miles away, in a rural area) and was told that in fact they had picked up a cocker spaniel and an Afghan hound the night before. I asked my neighbor if she would like for me to retrieve her dog as well. She was happy with my offer. I hopped in my little Volkswagen and drove to pick up the dogs.

After getting them "out of jail" and beginning the drive back home, I noticed that my car began sputtering... and sputtering... and then it stopped. In my worry and haste to get the dogs, I had failed to notice that my car's gas tank was nearly empty. I now was completely out of gas. There were no cell phones at that time, so I surmised I would need to walk to the nearest phone (which was quite a distance away) to summon help. Meanwhile, I had my dog (and the neighbor's dog, still in heat) sitting in the back seat of my little car. Agreeing to pick up both dogs in my little car was only the first stupid thing I did that day. I had not mentally or physically prepared myself for this journey. Not only had I failed to fill my tank, but now that I was on empty, havoc was preparing to rule.

I found some kind of restraint lying around my car (I'm not sure what kind—perhaps it was even dental floss!) and tied one dog to one door handle inside the car and the other dog to the other door handle. They began to howl. It was not a pretty sight or sound. I then ventured out (I think I was in tears at this point) to find some fuel. Fortunately, I was able to summon some help, and received enough fuel to make it to a gas station.

This describes how I felt today: out of gas and "on empty." I thought about the choices I had before me today. One choice was to get some much-needed rest (which I did). I remembered how Elijah had gone from an incredible day of great victory and rejoicing to feeling weak and discouraged the next day.

> He himself went a day's journey into the desert. He came to a broom tree, sat down under it and prayed that he might die. "I have had enough, LORD," he said. "Take my life; I am no better than my ancestors." Then he lay down under the tree and fell asleep.
> All at once an angel touched him and said, "Get up and eat." (1 Kings 19:4–5)

The rest and some nourishment helped. I then surmised I could choose to think about all things sad and borrow others' sorrows as well—or I could set my mind differently. (While it is good to feel compassion, when there is nothing I can do for a situation, I realize I simply need to take it to God.)

Most of all, I realized that I needed refueling. This meant I needed to humbly seek help and to search for a "filling station." It's not necessarily simple or quick to get to one. Sometimes we have to "tie up" the distractions in our back seat. Then we must "get out of the car" to find help leading us to a source of fuel. So, I decided to "tie up" the distractions that were howling in the back of my mind, and then searched for spiritual fuel. I was ministered to by the scriptures I read. I prayed to claim the promise in Ephesians 3:16:

> I pray that out of his glorious riches he may strengthen you with power through his Spirit in your inner being.

Then I read some more scriptures. It never ceases to amaze me how "alive and active" they are. I prayed that God would fill me up so I could give some more—and he did. I have been so very blessed by God. I know that if I imitate Jesus, it means I need to keep on giving and loving, even when I'm feeling tired of giving. Jesus did this again and again, no matter the circumstance. He amazes and inspires me. I'm so grateful that God, through his Spirit, continually fills us so that we can always have something to give.

> And hope does not disappoint us, because God has poured out his love into our hearts by the Holy Spirit, whom he has given us. (Romans 5:5)

why I don't like fishing   35

As I write this chapter, my husband is preparing sixty pounds of cod and haddock filets. Tomorrow night we will have a fish fry with our family group. The remainder will go to friends, family, and the freezer. Two days after Christmas, Wyndham went deep sea fishing and caught so many fish that his hands cramped from the strain of pulling them all in. (It might have also had something to do with being out on the ocean during winter in New England during high winds and four- to seven-foot waves.) He had a blast! I was so happy for him, and I have to say—the fish tastes pretty fantastic.

I wish I could enjoy this sport with him. However, if someone wanted to torture me, they could wake me up in the wee hours of the morning, load me on a boat, and take me fishing. No need to chum for fish... I'd automatically provide the chum. I can get sick just from looking at a wave.

It hasn't always been this way. When I was a young girl, I loved to fish for brim and bass in the pond in my back yard. I caught

111

fish on bread wads and bacon—and once in a while I even used bubble gum for bait. I never could handle the worms, though. They were just too slimy for me. I fished day after day, and loved it. However, something happened between then and now.

Today, I could enjoy about ten minutes of fishing if I was standing on the ground by a beautiful lake with the air temperature about seventy-two degrees Fahrenheit with a gentle breeze blowing to keep away the bugs. Someone else would need to bait my hook. I would need to catch a fish instantly, and then someone would have to take it off the hook for me and throw it back into the water. It would also be nice if a tasty picnic lunch was prepared to enjoy. I could munch on this while I stared at beautiful mountains in the background overlooking the lake. That would be okay.

But actually, I think I know what happened to my love of fishing. Shortly after we were married, I went deep sea fishing with Wyndham and his uncle (who loved fishing as much as Wyndham does). It was raining and the waves had deep swells. I quickly turned green and went down to the cabin in order to stay dry while I threw up. That proved to be a bad idea. My seasickness got worse and worse, so I ventured outside to sit in the rain and hurl over the side of the boat. As I sat down in the rain, Wyndham's uncle began chumming (putting whole fish guts and all into a meat grinder, then dumping them into the ocean to attract the fish). That was not helpful. He then gently put a tarp over me and assured me that we would turn back when the tide changed. (He was the boat captain, so he made the decisions.) When I learned that the tide would change in six hours, I seriously contemplated throwing myself overboard. Ever since that day, I have stayed far away from fishing. It was a fast and firm decision. I'm not even tempted to try it again. I don't want to get close to deep sea fishing—it made me completely miserable.

I thought about this when I read two scriptures today:

> Flee the evil desires of youth, and pursue righteousness, faith, love and peace, along with those who call on the Lord out of a pure heart. Don't have anything to do with foolish and stupid arguments, because you know they produce quarrels. (2 Timothy 2:22–23)

> Do not love the world or anything in the world. If anyone loves the world, the love of the Father is not in him. For everything in the world—the cravings of sinful man, the lust of his eyes and the boasting of what he has and does—comes not from the Father but from the world. The world and its desires pass away, but the man who does the will of God lives forever. (1 John 2:15–17)

Every day—from the alluring merchandise in the mall, to the television advertisements—the world tries to court us with money, things, pleasures, and all sorts of distractions from what really matters. Satan is chumming for our attention, and he wants us on his boat. That boat ride ends very badly. May I (and we) always remember how empty and deceitful the world really is, and stay as far away as possible—not setting foot on that boat. Rather, let us pursue righteousness, faith, love and peace, with a pure heart. These will not disappoint.

erasing "not possible" 36

I spent many years working for HOPE Worldwide in Romania, helping to organize a number of projects designed to help the local people. We organized the HOPE Youth Corps (a service camp for teens), built a home for orphans, and my family and I eventually adopted our son Jacob from Romania. As I met with people in Romania to work together on these projects, I often heard the same two words: "not possible."

The nation of Romania had suffered under a dictatorship for many years, and I believe that the dictatorship was to blame for this negative, defeated attitude. Even so, I still despised those two words. To me, that phrase sort of "puts its big toe over a line"—as if to dare me to try to go forward. These types of situations get my spiritual adrenaline going, because I know that God specializes in the impossible. When I hear "it's not possible," it somehow excites me to see what God might do.

I grew up with a dad who displayed on his desk a placard that read, "Now tell me all the reasons why it CAN be done." This exemplified to me his character and faith. I also remember a crazy

114

story about the time my oldest sister got a ticket for going down a one-way street the wrong way. Instead of paying a fine, she persuaded the court to change the road to become a two-way street! I have been inspired by the faith of so many people I have seen around me, and read so many accounts of real men and women in the Bible who stepped out on faith to witness God do the impossible. So I am well acquainted with examples of people who viewed obstacles and challenges as mere "hiccups."

More importantly, my spiritual father created the universe out of darkness and void, closed the mouths of lions, and drenched a parched land from a tiny cloud—just to mention a very few of his feats. He brought a nation of people from a closed womb, sent his Son to be born of a virgin, and then raised him from the dead. His finest work comes from the most unlikely and impossible situations.

Sometimes it takes tenacity, and sometimes it requires our stepping out of our comfort zone in order to be used by God to change a situation. I remember one particular (albeit insignificant) situation like this in my own life. I was pregnant with our first child and decided I wanted to stay (or get) in shape and take an exercise class. So I went to a neighborhood gym and inquired about joining a class for pregnant women. The manager gave me an inquisitive look and told me there was no such thing. I proceeded to convince him that this was a big mistake for their business, and they needed to offer such a class. In fact, they should pay me to teach it. Granted, I had no background in this and didn't know what I was doing. I looked ridiculous that day. I was wearing an old purple sweat suit (we had little money, so it had to suffice as my exercise wardrobe), and I looked like an Easter egg.

But by the end of the conversation, I had become the new instructor for the maternity aerobics class. I felt very out of my element, so I purchased Jane Fonda's videotape for pregnant women and did exactly what she did (well, at least I attempted to). I thrill at seeing possibilities unfold from "not possible" responses.

When faced with a situation that seems to have reached a dead end, it is certainly possible that God is simply saying no. However, it is also possible that he may want to use you or circumstances around you to change a seemingly impossible situation. In order to find out, it takes us stepping out on faith... most often out of our comfort zones.

What situations do you face that seem impossible to change... even when you know they need to change and it is within God's plan for them to change? What are some things that stretch your imagination as you envision them being different? Maybe it's seeing an obstacle overcome, changing something in your character, or healing a relationship. You may have numerous "not possibles" in your mind. As you think of them, consider the following scriptures:

> As it is written: "I have made you a father of many nations." He is our father in the sight of God, in whom he believed—the God who gives life to the dead and calls things that are not as though they were.
>
> Against all hope, Abraham in hope believed and so became the father of many nations, just as it had been said to him, "So shall your offspring be." Without weakening in his faith, he faced the fact that his body was as good as dead—since he was about a hundred years old—and that Sarah's womb was also dead. Yet he did not waver through unbelief regarding the promise of God, but was strengthened in his faith and gave glory to God, being fully persuaded that God had power to do what he had promised. (Romans 4:17–21)
>
> Now to him who is able to do immeasurably more than all we ask or imagine, according to his power that is at work within us, to him be glory in the church and in Christ Jesus throughout all generations, for ever and ever! Amen. (Ephesians 3:20–21)

What "not possibles" might you erase by trusting that God is able to do more than you dare ask or imagine?

what's your caption? 37

I happened upon this picture a few minutes ago. In this photo my granddaughter is having fun hiding behind a glass pulpit. I thought this photo communicated many things with just a few words.

If I were to put my face behind that glass, would the words shown in the picture—"To God Be the Glory"—reflect my life? I pray so. I desire the fruit of God's Spirit to be evident in my life so that God's glory can be seen and given honor. I love the thought of seeing each of our faces behind the glass of this picture... reflecting God's glory. *Glory* is sort of a "church word"—where the meaning can get lost in familiarity. I see *glory* most simply as the awesome (in the truest sense of the word) and consuming presence of God! Imagine with me your face behind this caption. Does it fit there? Do your expression and demeanor reflect God's presence? How about your words, and the tone of your words? Do the choices you are making reflect the glory of God? What would your caption say? Our demeanor, words, and choices always reflect something, and could always have an accompanying caption.

After reading many verses about God's glory, and pondering

the captions that could be applied to my life every day, I am more keenly equipped to consider what and whom I am reflecting as I go through my day. I'm also grateful, as the scripture below states, that God sees me as a work in progress, allowing me to grow and change each day. He is full of grace as well as truth, helping me in my weaknesses to become more like Jesus every day.

> But whenever anyone turns to the Lord, the veil is taken away. Now the Lord is the Spirit, and where the Spirit of the Lord is, there is freedom. And we, who with unveiled faces all reflect the Lord's glory, are being transformed into his likeness with ever-increasing glory, which comes from the Lord, who is the Spirit. (2 Corinthians 3:16–18)

Here is the same scripture, in the Message Bible:

> Whenever, though, they turn to face God as Moses did, God removes the veil and there they are—face to face! They suddenly recognize that God is a living, personal presence, not a piece of chiseled stone. And when God is personally present, a living Spirit, that old, constricting legislation is recognized as obsolete. We're free of it! All of us! Nothing between us and God, our faces shining with the brightness of his face. And so we are transfigured much like the Messiah, our lives gradually becoming brighter and more beautiful as God enters our lives and we become like him.

And here it is in the NRSV:

> But when one turns to the Lord, the veil is removed. Now the Lord is the Spirit, and where the Spirit of the Lord is, there is freedom. And all of us, with unveiled faces, seeing the glory of the Lord as though reflected in a mirror, are being transformed into the same image from one degree of glory to another; for this comes from the Lord, the Spirit.

the power of music   38

Have you ever thought how different a movie would be without its soundtrack? Watching the scenes without musical accompaniment would be sort of like eating food without flavor. I truly enjoy great soundtracks; however, I've had to train my ear to hear them well. So often, I have just taken them for granted, unaware of the mood that they are helping to produce. We can usually know when something scary is going to happen, or when someone is falling in love, based on the score in the background. I've also come to realize the contributing role that music plays in my emotions.

If I may wax philosophical for a moment, I'll share a quote attributed to Plato: "Music is a moral law. It gives a soul to the universe, wings to the mind, flight to the imagination, a charm to sadness, and life to everything. It is the essence of order, and leads to all that is good, just and beautiful, of which it is the invisible, but nevertheless dazzling, passionate, and eternal form."[1]

God's creation exudes harmony. To me, the wind, the waves, the streams, the birds, the thunder, and the crackling of a fire are all parts of this orchestra.

---

1. *Wordsworth Dictionary of Musical Quotations*, comp. Derek Watson (Ware, Hertsfordshire: Wordsworth Editions Ltd.,1991), p. 45.

> You will go out in joy
>   and be led forth in peace;
> the mountains and hills will burst into song before you,
> and all the trees of the field will clap their hands.
> (Isaiah 55:12)

Somehow, God's presence within us has the ability to soothe, to comfort and express love—much as a mother does when singing to her child.

> By day the LORD directs his love,
>   at night his song is with me—
>   a prayer to the God of my life. (Psalm 42:8)

As I read scriptures about songs, I found that they were used in so many ways:

To awaken (Judges 5:12); to celebrate victory (Psalm 18:1–2); to express joy and praise (Psalm 28:7); to express love (Isaiah 5:1); to alleviate fear (Isaiah 12:2); to find comfort (Isaiah 49:13); to mourn (Micah 2:4); and the list goes on.

I realize that my personal playlists of songs reflect so many of these areas. I have greatly increased my use of music over the past year. I find it helpful in setting my mind. There are songs I like to wake up to, such as "What a Wonderful World," "You Raise Me Up," and "Light Your World," to name a few. Some songs help me feel close to God (they are on my Quiet Time playlist), some inspire me and help me exercise, and then there are some (my dancing music playlist) that help me dance through the kitchen and laundry room. I have some that comfort me (such as "Be Still My Soul" and "Abide with Me"). I try to stay away from dirges that bring me down (although I do have quite a long country playlist that I enjoy).

Some of my favorites are playing as I write. I enjoy some nice background music (with a fair shake of Kenny G and Il Volo.) I like to keep these songs playing in the background when I'm at home.

A philosopher (some have also attributed this quote to Plato) once said, "Let me handle the music for one generation and I will control Rome." In other words, the things we listen to and allow into our minds affect our thoughts and actions. It makes sense to me, in order to help "set my mind on things above," to listen to music that agrees with this desire.

Give it a try. You may be surprised at the lift that songs bring to your heart, and the pep they put in your step.

oh, my! what did I get myself into?!   39

Have you ever been faced with a decision you made, and later thought, "What in the world was I thinking?" Last night, as I packed a travel crate, blanket, and puppy collar, I felt a bit of fear and trepidation. In fact, I felt more than a bit. You see, dog life has gotten quite easy over here. Our little ten-year-old "cockerpoo" (a cockerpoo is what you get when a cocker spaniel and a poodle get married!) goes out once in the morning and then again at night. We don't even have to walk outside with him if the weather is bad. Meanwhile, he just wanders from the sofa to his little bed, circling each place a few times until he settles on the best spot for a nap.

Wyndham leaves for a meeting this afternoon and plans to come back in a couple of days with a little something inside that travel crate: an eight-week-old puppy full of life and energy. I have found myself wondering why in the world I agreed to this—what insanity entered my mind to do this puppy thing again? My "easy dog life" is about to be over. I must confess, I am feeling a slight sense of panic.

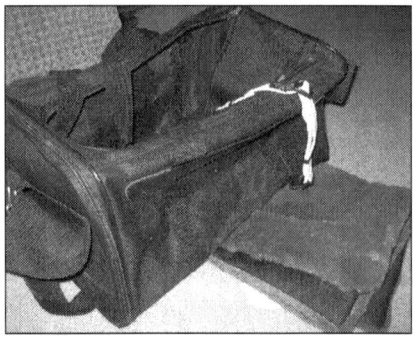

In my future, I am seeing several weeks of puddles and worse—perhaps a chewed chair leg or two, along with some mangled toys that were intended for the grandchildren's play. I'm sure there will be lots of hair for daily vacuuming, vet bills, and—if we are fortunate to have many years with him—another heartbreak, twelve to fourteen years from now.

So why in the world would I do this?

Because I envision the sheer joy he will lavish upon me when I come in the door after being gone; the eagerness he will have to please us; his ability to love unconditionally; his longing eyes and cute antics; his energy and zeal; his head that will rest on my knee; and most of all, his devotion as a loyal friend... All this will make it worth it. Dog ownership is really about the relationship between a man and his dog and a woman and her dog.

So, having already made a deposit for the puppy, I just wrote a check for the remainder of the payment. I sighed a bit, but then smiled. To us, he will be more than worth the cost. We weighed the decision and considered it long and hard. I'm sort of glad we had to put a deposit down. This helped me keep my resolve. When something doesn't cost me anything, I am more apt to back out. I made a wholehearted decision. If I had kept wavering in indecision I would be miserable, and I would fail to enjoy this soon-to-be reality of a new puppy. I can already feel his cuteness.

On a far weightier matter, I made a decision many years ago, when I was a teenager, to become a Christian—a follower of Jesus. Since I came out of the waters of baptism, there have been many exhilarating times, and numerous challenges, victories, and defeats. I wouldn't trade this life for anything. I made a big decision to turn my life over to Jesus' care and direction, yet he made the far bigger deposit: his life. That deposit, and the one he gave me of his Spirit living in me, has helped me keep my resolve to follow Jesus—with no turning back!

> Then he said to them all: "If anyone would come after me, he must deny himself and take up his cross daily and follow me. For whoever wants to save his life will lose it, but whoever loses his life for me will save it. What good is it for a man to gain the whole world, and yet lose or forfeit his very self?" (Luke 9:23–25)

> Jesus replied, "No one who puts his hand to the plow and looks back is fit for service in the kingdom of God."
> (Luke 9:62)

A decision to turn back would not only cost my salvation, but would also affect others who see my life. Most of all, I would miss out on the most amazing benefit of this decision: a relationship with God who gives me forgiveness, friendship, family, purpose, identity, acceptance, fullness of life, and so much more.

This relationship has such an amazing effect on all of my other relationships. I love this relationship that I "got myself into"!

Denver's coming! 40

Tomorrow is a big day. Yes, Denver is coming to town for a big playoff football game against the New England Patriots. But more importantly, my husband is flying through Denver, Colorado, to pick up our new puppy, Denver. Look at that face! He just makes you want to hug him, doesn't he?

After getting over my episode of sheer terror at the thought of raising a new puppy again, I'm really excited. I feel like a kid on Christmas Eve. I can't wait to meet the little guy. I am sure he has no idea what is about to happen to him. He will leave his familiar place—his mom and his siblings. (Now I feel like I want to cry.) He will be transferred to the hands of a man he hasn't met and go on a long airplane ride in a soft crate under my husband's seat. It may be a bit traumatic. It's sort of like a new birth. He will likely wonder what new world he is entering into, and he must entrust himself to his new owner.

However, what he doesn't know is what is waiting for him on the "other side." I've been preparing a place for him. He's got the Cadillac of dog crates, new toys, a new collar, puppy treats, some big brothers, a family of adults and children who can't wait to shower their love on him, and a promise of care, training, and lots and lots of love. It's going to be a good life. We can't wait for him to get here.

I thought of this same type of transition to a new place when my grandchildren were born. They were at one time safe, warm, and snuggly inside their mother's womb. However, little did they know that on the "other side" waiting for them were parents and grandparents, aunts and uncles who already loved them. And there were hugs, kisses, and even (as I had with three of my grandchildren tonight) pizza, brownies, and ice cream in their futures as well. That's got to be much tastier than anything the umbilical cord offers.

I can't help but wonder if this is something like God feels as he awaits his children's arrival—from their "new birth" all the way until heaven. He must shake his head at how attached we can get to this world, scared to let go; and our fear of trusting him. All the while we have no idea that "amazing awaits"—on the other side.

> However, as it is written:
>
> "No eye has seen,
>   no ear has heard,
> no mind has conceived
>   what God has prepared for those who love him."
> (1 Corinthians 2:9)
>
> "Do not let your hearts be troubled. Trust in God; trust also in me. In my Father's house are many rooms; if it were not so, I would have told you. I am going there to prepare a place for you. And if I go and prepare a place for you, I will come back and take you to be with me that you also may be where I am. You know the way to the place where I am going."
>
> Thomas said to him, "Lord, we don't know where you are going, so how can we know the way?"
>
> Jesus answered, "I am the way and the truth and the life. No one comes to the Father except through me. If you really knew me, you would know my Father as well. From now on, you do know him and have seen him."
> (John 14:1–7)

up close and personal   41

I'm finally holding our fluffy fur ball, and I'm in love. We now have our new puppy "in person." We've anticipated this new adventure for a while. The little guy is now no longer an idea or a plan. Although I had received pictures via email and text, and had a bit of information about him, I'm no longer connected to him via cyberspace. I'm grateful for that.

Technology always falls short when relationships are involved, as there is no substitute for being together. I needed to see the twinkle in his eyes, smell his puppy breath, feel his nibbling on my nose, and participate in the sacrifice of taking him out at three in the morning to really feel connected. Suffice it to say, I'm connected.

How much more important it is to have our human connections "up close and personal." There truly is no substitute for "being there." While I am grateful for the many tools that make some kind of connection to people possible, I have come to realize that they can never substitute for a personal touch, a hug, looking someone in the eyes, hearing their words or sighs, and seeing their expressions. There is no substitute for holding hands in prayer around a dinner table, expressing our thoughts to a listening ear, being a listening ear for someone else's concerns, reading and studying the Bible together, praying together, sharing appreciation, and talking across a table. These take "up close and personal" interaction. While an email can be quickly sent, it is often difficult to know the heart that is behind it. Texts r snt almost w/o thot.

God knew we needed to be "up close and personal." Otherwise, we just have religion and fail to understand what a relationship with God is all about. What an amazing, implausible expression of love God has given us in Jesus, who left heaven and came to live and be with us.

> The Word became flesh and made his dwelling among us. We have seen his glory, the glory of the One and Only, who came from the Father, full of grace and truth.
> (John 1:14)

> This is how God showed his love among us: He sent his one and only Son into the world that we might live through him. (1 John 4:9)

These scriptures amaze me. I so desperately need this kind of love so that I can better understand God and his will for my life. Because he came here "up close and personal," I can see what he did, what he said, how he prayed, how he lived, and how he died.

> To this you were called, because Christ suffered for you, leaving you an example, that you should follow in his steps. (1 Peter 2:21)

Though Jesus' physical presence in this world lasted for a mere thirty-three years, it has impacted me forever. Today, it is still very real. I can feel and know his presence in my life.

While I hope the little personal stories I share can help the Scriptures come alive, the personal stories are just that: personal stories. It is the Scriptures that are really profound. As I read this next scripture, I am reminded again of the intense privilege and responsibility that go into a relationship with God, and am so deeply appreciative for his "up close and personal" love.

> "If you love me, you will obey what I command. And I will ask the Father, and he will give you another Counselor to be with you forever—the Spirit of truth. The world cannot accept him, because it neither sees him nor knows him. But you know him, for he lives with you and will be in you. I will not leave you as orphans; I will come to you. Before long, the world will not see me anymore, but you will see me. Because I live, you also will live. On that day you will realize that I am in my Father, and you are in me, and I am in you. Whoever has my commands and obeys them, he is the one who loves me. He who loves me will be loved by my Father, and I too will love him and show myself to him." (John 14:15–21)

Yes, I'm connected to Denver, and I already love him. However, there is nothing comparable to having God's presence "up close and personal" in my life.

leaving a mark 42

As I prepare to write, I stand amazed at how quickly and thoroughly our new puppy has impact wherever he goes. In about ten seconds' time he has chewed a box, tried to pull out the computer wire, chomped on the trash can, brought out a towel, carried papers away—and that's just half of the list of his "accomplishments"! I am confident that Denver leaves a mark every place he visits, although it's not always a positive one. (It's a good thing he's so cute.)

While he is still a baby, and not yet trained, this tiny little fur ball can alter numerous situations around him quite quickly and decisively. It is dumbfounding to me. (I'm also becoming a strong advocate for crate training.)

I pray, as I go about my day today, that I can "leave a mark"—a good one—on people and situations around me. I am confident that this can't happen without prayer, thought, focus, and initiative.

> Let us hold unswervingly to the hope we profess, for he who promised is faithful. And **let us consider** how we may spur one another on toward love and good deeds. (Hebrews 10:23–24, emphasis added)

If I am not alert to the presence of God in my life, I am likely to go through the day leaving little or no mark. I can sometimes be like a phrase I once heard, "Sometimes I sit and think, and sometimes I just sit."

One of my friends, when I was a young Christian, used to greet me excitedly, saying, "Did you have a Jesus day? Did you have some Jesus conversations?" This would always get me thinking, because when I consider the life of Jesus, and read again and again the accounts of his life, I am utterly amazed by him, and called so much higher. Everywhere Jesus went, every person he spoke to, every situation he was in, he made a difference. He left a mark.

The sick were healed, and "casual conversations" with Jesus led to decisions that altered people's eternity. When Jesus spoke with individuals, they felt heard, understood, loved, and often very challenged. Jesus spoke with authority. He also cried with compassion. He was dependent upon his relationship with the Father. He spoke the truth that resonated with hurting, troubled, and complacent hearts. He made huge "dinner parties" from mere leftovers, and kept his focus on what was truly important rather than on what seemed urgent. Jesus showed us what love really means. He did this in an unparalleled way: by giving his own life for those who disregarded him and spat in his face—including me. Yes, I am amazed. I pray I can leave some life-changing mark today that reflects Jesus in me and points someone to him.

> "In the same way, let your light shine before men, that they may see your good deeds and praise your Father in heaven." (Matthew 5:16)

> Whoever claims to live in him must walk as Jesus did.
> (1 John 2:6)

Yes, our new puppy leaves a mark everywhere he goes. Like him, I pray to leave more of a mark wherever I go. I pray the mark I leave will be more like Jesus than Denver. I long to carry Jesus to situations and conversations I encounter, one person at a time.

And whatever you do, whether in word or deed, do it all in the name of the Lord Jesus, giving thanks to God the Father through him. (Colossians 3:17)

May the God of peace, who through the blood of the eternal covenant brought back from the dead our Lord Jesus, that great Shepherd of the sheep, equip you with everything good for doing his will, and may he work in us what is pleasing to him, through Jesus Christ, to whom be glory for ever and ever. Amen. (Hebrews 13:20–21)

the annoyed older brother   43

Our older dog hates Denver. Okay, I'll put it out there and call the disgruntled dog by his name: Blackie. Let me begin with a disclaimer. I love our older dog, but I don't like his name. His name was left to the discretion of our youngest son, who (being from another country) still had a limited English vocabulary at the time. He was given this dog for Christmas ten years ago and wanted to name him Blackie. I tried to persuade him otherwise, but he was determined. Our African-American friends sometime give us a hard time (all in fun) about his name. I am, however, unsure if this name might be offensive to people I don't know.

When I call for him to come in from the park across the street he answers to the "public" name I gave him: Jackie. It works. If he stubbornly procrastinates, I add a surname: "You come here, Jackie Chan!" So now I have finished the disclaimer and can tell you in truth that Blackie despises Denver.

Blackie navigates a routine throughout his day-to-day activities. He has a path he travels each morning, a place for his naps, and he occasionally throws a ball in the air. He goes out at night and comes back to beg for his treat. He is obedient (most of the time) and is very easy to care for. He is independent, and to me, caring for him is sort of like operating on autopilot. Life has been good for Blackie, even though he went through several weeks of adjustment after Jordan died.

And then... we interrupted his life with a "little brother." Blackie quickly set the pecking order with the new pup: Denver takes a fully submissive posture (on his back) when Blackie the alpha dog cruises by. As Blackie approaches Denver, it's as if he deliberately moves in slow motion, with a look of utter disgust—almost as if he wishes to throw up.

I guess he sees Denver as an unnecessary nuisance, unwanted competition, and an annoying distraction to his routine. I hope that time will fill the "older brother" with some affection for the adorable little guy. Meanwhile, I try to be patient as I try to persuade Blackie to let Denver into his heart and life.

While it may seem really selfish and arrogant for Blackie to act this way, I realize how easy it is for me to "growl" and feel annoyed when my routine is interrupted by something or someone. I am once again challenged when I read about Jesus, particularly in the events of Mark 6. Jesus had tragically lost his friend and relative, John. John had been brutally killed. Jesus was certainly heartbroken. Following this event, we read this account:

> The apostles gathered around Jesus and reported to him all they had done and taught. Then, because so many people were coming and going that they did not even have a chance to eat, he said to them, "Come with me by yourselves to a quiet place and get some rest."
> So they went away by themselves in a boat to a solitary place. But many who saw them leaving recognized them and ran on foot from all the towns and got there ahead of them. When Jesus landed and saw a large crowd, he had compassion on them, because they were like sheep without a shepherd. So he began teaching them many things. (Mark 6:30–34)

I pray to be more like Jesus each day. To keep on giving when I want to "stride past and growl" because my routine and comfort have been interrupted; to let others in when I feel my plate is full; and to be full of compassion when I'm tired or sad, and yet someone is in need.

I can't hear you! 44

I rattled the dish, ever so quietly, and Denver came running over, thinking it was time to be fed. This little puppy devours his food in a matter of seconds, with what seems like one gulp. The slightest crumpling of a bag or rattling of a dish sends him into a whirlwind. He responds immediately, almost running over himself to get to the food.

At other times, I can call loudly for him to come to me. I can also look at him and tell him, "Denver, no, don't eat my boot...

or the computer wire... or the chair... or my ear"—and he suddenly becomes deaf. Here you can see him listening so well as he is chomping on my boot: Granted, he is only nine weeks old and still untrained, but I am quite sure his hearing is fine. It's not that he can't hear me, or connect that the word "no" has repercussions associated with it. At this point, in his immature state, it seems he hears only what he wants to hear. We are teaching him basic commands as quickly as possible, for his own safety (and our sanity). This makes me think about how easy it is for us as humans to hear "conveniently," as Denver does.

Think about things you are eager to hear. You may await a certain phone call, or thrill at the sound of a child or grandchild as they utter their first words. I think about times I have been eager to hear good news of someone's safe arrival, or to hear the voice of a loved one.

I ask myself how eager I am to hear the words of my God. Do I strain in eager anticipation in order to hear them, or do I merely listen "at my convenience"? The answer can be found in my daily habits. Do I eagerly open pages of my Bible (or open Bible applications on my computer)? Do I really want to hear what God has to say to me? Or will I glance through the Bible at my leisure—at my convenience?

What keeps us from eagerly listening for and hearing the words of God? What causes us to stumble over them and not take them to heart? There can be various reasons, but perhaps the most common is what I observe with my puppy: He is so busy doing what he wants to do that he doesn't care to listen.

As 1 Peter 2:8 says, "They stumble because they disobey the message." It's easy to be careless with listening, and it's easy to stumble with the Scriptures when we don't want to do what they say. That's like Denver, when he doesn't want to obey. I am always sobered by the scripture in Hebrews 2:1–3:

> We must pay more careful attention, therefore, to what we have heard, so that we do not drift away. For if the message spoken by angels was binding, and every violation and disobedience received its just punishment, how shall we escape if we ignore such a great salvation? This salvation, which was first announced by the Lord, was confirmed to us by those who heard him.

Listen carefully... what do you hear?

is God under "they-a"? 45

My granddaughter Lexi, who is two and a half years old, was "reading" with her mom yesterday morning. As in any household with three children, quiet moments are few and far between. The two older children had gone off to school, and Lexi sat with her mommy as Melissa read the Bible. As Lexi went off to play, Melissa put a blanket over her head to drown out the noise and distractions surrounding her. This is how she, at times, creates her own personal "prayer closet."

As could be expected, Lexi came over to her mommy and lifted up the blanket to ask why she had the blanket over her head. Melissa explained to her that she was praying and was just trying to keep the surrounding sounds muffled so that she could concentrate.

"Oh," Lexi answered, and went back to her play.

She soon came back to Melissa, lifted up the blanket again, and in her New England accent asked, "Is God under 'they-a?'" ("They-a" is the New England way to say "there.")

I am so grateful that the answer to that question is a resounding "Yes!" God is under "they-a," and he is also over "he-a" ("here," to the non-locals) with me! He will be found by everyone who seeks him wholeheartedly. I thrill to the knowledge that he encompasses a dimension that is far beyond 3–D. The dimension he covers is one that works its way into the depths of our inner being—our heart and soul. I am encouraged to know that "the eyes of the LORD range throughout the earth to strengthen those whose hearts are fully committed to him" (2 Chronicles 16:9).

God is not only here with me, but he came looking for me, and is looking to strengthen all those whose hearts are fully his.

I'm also grateful for his presence in my life... as I go to my appointments and meetings, shop for groceries, travel, and lay my head down at night. He goes with me.

> Yet I am always with you;
>   you hold me by my right hand.
> You guide me with your counsel,
>   and afterward you will take me into glory.
> Whom have I in heaven but you?
>   And earth has nothing I desire besides you.
> My flesh and my heart may fail,
>   but God is the strength of my heart
>   and my portion forever. (Psalm 73:23–26)

The picture above may look like a simple lump under a blanket. However, when prayer (the act of talking to the God of the universe, our creator—wow!) happens under there or anywhere else, there is a spiritual energy and reality at work that can't be seen by the naked eye (even with 3–D glasses). My mind cannot fathom the workings of God that can be moved by prayer and time in the Word, but I see the results day after day.

> "For my thoughts are not your thoughts,
>   neither are your ways my ways," declares the LORD.
> "As the heavens are higher than the earth,
>   so are my ways higher than your ways
>   and my thoughts than your thoughts.
> As the rain and the snow

come down from heaven,
and do not return to it
 without watering the earth
and making it bud and flourish,
 so that it yields seed for the sower and bread for the
  eater,
so is my word that goes out from my mouth:
 It will not return to me empty,
 but will accomplish what I desire
 and achieve the purpose for which I sent it.
You will go out in joy
 and be led forth in peace;
the mountains and hills
 will burst into song before you,
and all the trees of the field
 will clap their hands." (Isaiah 55:8–12)

obedience is underrated 46

Obedience training has begun. My husband is working with our little pup, teaching him four basic commands: sit, stay, come, and no. These are the commands that, when Denver is fully trained, he should respond to immediately—and always. I look forward to his increased obedience as he matures. He will not only be more pleasant to live with, but he will be much safer. I will be able to count on stopping him before he runs out into the road, or swallows a toy, or eats a shoe. I can know he will come in when he is called, so he won't get lost. Basic obedience will also allow him to fulfill the "work" he is  bred to do: upland hunting. When he finds pheasant in the field in a few months, he will likely experience the joy of doing the job for which he was created. I see very clearly with Denver how obedience is taught, learned, and practiced over and over again.

I smile as I watch my grandchildren learn obedience. It's a beautiful thing. As an adult, it's easy to look at children's stubbornness and disobedience and think, "Come on, just surrender and do what's right. It will be so much easier, so much better than fighting the 'war' in which you are engaging."

I can only imagine how often God has felt that way about me! Yet I take comfort in knowing that Jesus understands that obedience is often hard. He, though perfect, had to learn obedience. He learned through many trials. As it says in Hebrews 5:8, "Although he was a son, he learned obedience from what he suffered."

When children learn obedience (through what they suffer), they (and others around them) are always so much happier afterward. I love my grandchildren! They are so much fun, and they are great kids. I had to laugh as I heard about the antics of my youngest grandson, Micah, a few days ago. Micah has such a sweet, tender conscience, and can carry on conversations way beyond his (almost) two years of age. However, as he nears the age of two, this struggle for obedience can be humorous to watch.

Earlier this week he said no to his dad. That, of course, was not acceptable. His daddy then told him he was not to tell daddy no, and that if he did he would be punished. Micah then looked away from his dad, found his mommy's eyes, and calmly said, "No, Mommy!" He just wanted to "clarify" (or test) what it meant to be obedient.

And sometimes, our obedience is outward, without being inward. After Micah's mom told him that he could not watch the movie *The Polar Express* again since he had already watched it that day, Micah walked away mumbling under his breath, "I *will* watch *Pola Press*; I *can* watch *Pola Press*!" Obedience is often hard. That's why it's called obedience. If it wasn't difficult, it could just be called "doing what we want to do." We can, like Micah, do the right thing, but it can take a while for our attitudes to catch up to our actions. This is a good place to start, however!

This principle was further illustrated by a conversation I had with a dear friend last week. She had struggled for a while with feeling surrendered to God after experiencing several difficult situations. She simply could not find much joy in her walk with God. However, she kept walking.

Several months ago, she was able to regain her joy in her relationships, beginning with her relationship with God. The change in her attitude is evident in her conversations, her expression, and her entire demeanor. She is able to think and process without the angst that was previously there. I asked her what had brought her this newfound peace.

Her answer was simply, "You know, obedience is underrated." She went on to explain that in her struggle, she had maintained her love and respect (her fear of God), and had decided that she would be obedient to God and his word despite how she felt. It was not always smooth, but she kept on doing the things that were right. In time, God blessed that obedience and she found her "heart" again.

The Scriptures state this reality in Philippians 2:12–13:

> Therefore, my dear friends, as you have always obeyed—not only in my presence, but now much more in my absence—continue to work out your salvation with fear and trembling, for it is God who works in you to will and to act according to his good purpose.

If we keep on obeying, out of awe for God, he will give us the will (the "want to," the "heart") to carry out his purposes for which we were created. When we don't feel like doing this, continual obedience to God will take us through the "muck and mire" and lead our hearts to the "other side." There, as with Denver and my grandchildren, we will be safe, happy, and able to fulfill the purposes for which we were created.

Never underrate simple obedience.

de-dreading the dentist   47

I strongly dislike going to the dentist. Yesterday I had my semiannual appointment to get my teeth cleaned. (I was six months late scheduling this appointment, so it actually became my annual appointment.) It's far too easy to procrastinate when it comes to doing things I don't enjoy. Fortunately, thus far my teeth haven't given me problems, and I still have them—wisdom and all. I'm grateful I didn't have to go to a "tooth cleaning"!

When I'm dreading a task, I try to add some redeeming quality to make it better. I think about the apostle Paul in these situations. His attitude continually convicts and inspires me. While in prison because of his faith, he wrote about continually rejoicing, encouraging others, and finding the unseen blessings in his trials. These blessings included his ability to share about Jesus with people he might not have had the opportunity to meet were it not for his difficult circumstances.

> Now I want you to know, brothers, that what has happened to me has really served to advance the gospel. As a result, it has become clear throughout the whole palace guard and to everyone else that I am in chains for Christ. Because of my chains, most of the brothers in the Lord have been encouraged to speak the word of God more courageously and fearlessly....
>
> Yes, and I will continue to rejoice, for I know that through your prayers and the help given by the Spirit of Jesus Christ, what has happened to me will turn out for my deliverance. I eagerly expect and hope that I will in no way be ashamed, but will have sufficient courage so that now as always Christ will be exalted in my body, whether by life or by death. (Philippians 1:12–14, 18–20)

Wow. These words call me higher. I wonder what my letter might have sounded like if I were in Paul's situation.

So as I went to the dentist's office, trying to learn from my brother Paul, I looked for opportunities to share, to encourage, and to rejoice and be thankful in a situation I didn't like. (Of course, going to the dentist and being in prison are not at all comparable, but I do really, really dread going to the dentist!) Regardless, by applying these scriptural principles to my mundane situation, it made the experience so much better. In fact, I almost enjoyed the time. My dentist practices in a town near the ocean. So before I subjected myself to the lovely sound of metal-on-plaque, I took a few extra minutes to pick up a cup of my favorite fish chowder in Gloucester, and then drove to my favorite prayer spot to enjoy my chowder and pray. This was the view from my car.

Truthfully, I believe God's beauty can be found everywhere, when we are looking. Yes, this is a magnificent view, but so are the stars—and the trees, the flowers, the animals—everything he has made. I made it through my dentist appointment, and even attempted to "enjoy" the few moments when I was able to close my eyes and listen to music (even with the occasional instrumental accompaniment of the dental tools).

There are numerous other "tasks" I don't enjoy. I don't like to iron or put away clothes. But years ago, a sister taught me to pray with thankfulness for the family member for whom I was ironing. This helped. I don't mind ironing anymore. Well at least not as much as I did. (Fortunately I don't have to do it so often now.) I tire of the daily ritual of washing my hair. Yet I take this time to think about what I've learned and can share—and new chapters for books are born. For some reason, my thoughts come best then, so I've learned to look forward to the time. The decisions I make about my attitude really do make a difference in my feelings toward the necessary but unpleasant tasks I encounter.

May we all learn from Paul in the Scriptures as we look for ways to rejoice, to encourage, to see God at work, and to find new opportunities to share about Jesus as we sit in our proverbial dentist chairs.

kicking trees 48

When as a young girl I got mad, frustrated, or began whining, my mother gave me words of wisdom. At the time I didn't know they were words of wisdom. I just thought her words of instruction were normal protocol.

Her instruction was this: "Go outside, run around the house six times, and kick some trees." So, I would go outside, count as I ran around the house, and kick one of the big pine trees in our backyard. I always felt better after this exercise.

I thought about this several times this week. One of my oft-used scriptures is short but profound. It is found in Romans 12:21: "Do not be overcome by evil, but overcome evil with good."

What an important scripture to practice. I have learned that I can find success in overcoming sin, temptations, or even annoying habits by applying this verse. All those years ago, my mother was actually training me to replace what was bad with something good. (The exercise was good and helped me get rid of my frustration... and no trees were harmed in this process.)

It's sort of like this: Imagine if you decided that you ate too much chocolate (is that possible?), so you decided to quit eating it for a while. You might then think about how you would need to avoid all Lindt dark chocolate bars with a sprinkling of chili in them. You might ponder the fact that by no means would you indulge in a molten chocolate cake, warm from the oven with melted Ghirardelli chocolate oozing out of the center, all smothered in ice cream. And certainly you would no longer order a Wendy's Frosty and enjoy slow tastes of the cold, creamy chocolate that coats your throat in an oh-so-palatable way.

Needless to say, thinking these thoughts would not be a smart way to get chocolate out of your life. Even as I write this while I sit in a neighborhood coffee shop, I am tempted to indulge in the chocolate goodies staring at me from behind the glass. You see, God knows that the way to overcome a temptation is to replace it with something else. What I need to do now is take a walk or eat an apple!

Jesus taught this truth with a parable:

> "When an evil spirit comes out of a man, it goes through arid places seeking rest and does not find it. Then it says, 'I will return to the house I left.' When it arrives, it finds the house swept clean and put in order. Then it goes and takes seven other spirits more wicked than itself, and they go in and live there. And the final condition of that man is worse than the first." (Luke 11:24–26)

Too often we try to get rid of besetting sins or bad habits by "sweeping our house clean" without then filling it with godly attributes, actions, and thoughts. Some practical ways to do this can be found in Colossians 3:

> Put to death, therefore, whatever belongs to your earthly nature: sexual immorality, impurity, lust, evil desires and greed, which is idolatry. Because of these, the wrath of God is coming. You used to walk in these ways, in the life you once lived. But now you must rid yourselves of all such things as these: anger, rage, malice, slander, and filthy language from your lips. Do not lie to each other, since you have taken off your old self with its practices and have put on the new self, which is being renewed in knowledge in the image of its Creator....

> Therefore, as God's chosen people, holy and dearly loved, clothe yourselves with compassion, kindness, humility, gentleness and patience. Bear with each other and forgive whatever grievances you may have against one another. Forgive as the Lord forgave you. And over all these virtues put on love, which binds them all together in perfect unity.
> Let the peace of Christ rule in your hearts, since as members of one body you were called to peace. And be thankful. (Colossians 3:5–10, 12–15)

A few days ago I was reading Romans 12:21 with a young woman who was eager to become a Christian. She wanted help in overcoming some destructive habits, so she decided to "arm herself" with several scriptures that she could immediately turn to, along with prayer. She also found support from a few sisters whom she could call when she faced temptation. She decided to begin these practices in order to "overcome evil with good." She was thrilled to learn of the promise that God's Spirit would enter her when she was baptized. She was learning to put off evil and put on good, and *to* overcome rather than to *be* overcome.

What a privilege to have the resources to overcome evil instead of being overcome by evil. What trees do you need to kick today?

my, how things change!   49

We were pulling into Boston, with our car fully packed. The year was 1987 and we were driving to what would become our new home. We had our three children in tow, one dog, and a few belongings. We wondered what this new chapter of our life would bring to our family. I looked back at the children and noticed that our usually happy Sam, then four years old, was quite melancholy. I asked him what was wrong. His reply took me by surprise.

Let me give you some background before I tell you his reply. At four years old, Sam was already good at entertaining himself. Although the children didn't watch a lot of television, they did have a few favorite shows. I had thought that Sam would enjoy the usual *Sesame Street*-type of program. However, he had no interest in such shows. Sam, even as a toddler, was mesmerized by anything having to do with sports. I can still picture him in his high chair joyfully watching football. By the time he was four years old, he knew a lot about sports, even sports trivia.

And so I should not have been surprised at Sam's response as we approached our new home. He answered with a sigh: "Oh no, now I have to be a Patriots fan." Our little four-year-old realized that his move came with the price of a new sports allegiance. He had been struggling with the inevitable fact that he would now need to become an official fan of a new team. Unfortunately, during those years the New England Patriots were, in a word, horrendous.

During the next several years, New England Patriots paraphernalia was amazingly cheap because they were such a bad team. It was not encouraging to be a Patriots fan. My, how things can change over time! This team went from worst to first (or second... I'm still a little tender from our 2012 loss in the Super Bowl). To this day, my grown-up son and his daughter are loyal Patriots fans.

I find there is a spiritual lesson for me to learn in most every situation I encounter, including this one. My young son was extremely discouraged about his new sports team. While that was certainly not an important issue in the grand scheme of life, we are all faced with disappointing or difficult situations or circumstances throughout our lives. Some are minor annoyances and some are major obstacles. Sometimes we encounter situations, circumstances, or weaknesses in our lives that can bring about great discouragement. We can be tempted to think that God put these things in our lives to bring us down; however, this is far from the truth. Consider the following scriptures:

> We do not want you to be uninformed, brothers, about the hardships we suffered in the province of Asia. We were under great pressure, far beyond our ability to endure, so that we despaired even of life. Indeed, in our hearts we felt the sentence of death. But this happened that we might not rely on ourselves but on God, who raises the dead. (2 Corinthians 1:8–9)

Paul experienced severe hardships as he followed Jesus. His trials caused him to rely on God. How easy it is when things go well to become self-reliant and less mindful of our utter dependence on God for every breath we take. We need our difficulties to remind us to rely on God.

The next scripture has often encouraged me, as it promises that my weaknesses can one day become my strengths:

> To keep me from becoming conceited because of these surpassingly great revelations, there was given me a thorn in my flesh, a messenger of Satan, to torment me. Three times I pleaded with the Lord to take it away from me. But he said to me, "My grace is sufficient for you, for my power is made perfect in weakness." Therefore I will boast all the more gladly about my weaknesses, so that Christ's power may rest on me. That is why, for Christ's sake, I delight in weaknesses, in insults, in hardships, in persecutions, in difficulties. For when I am weak, then I am strong.
> (2 Corinthians 12:7–10)

So I figure if I hang in there with true faith, any difficult situation can become one that helps me grow and brings glory to God. True joy and delight come from the reality that regardless of my situation, my *perspective* can always change!

the red *X* 50

For days now—months, actually— I've driven by these two trees, each marked with a big red *X* on its trunk. I've wondered if the markings were graffiti, if the trees were diseased and needed treatment, or if they were perhaps marked for cutting. However, I surmised that if they were to be cut down, they would not need large red *X*s to distinguish them, as they were the only trees in this particular front yard.

Each time I drive by those trees I become more curious. They were obviously singled out—but why? What did they do to deserve this big red *X*? Why were they chosen?

After driving by this site so many times, I decided to take a picture of these trees, as they were beginning to teach me lessons. I found myself thinking of spiritual lessons each time I cruised by. Armed with my camera, I pulled into the driveway beside the trees and rolled down the window of my car. The wind was blowing and I heard a sweet, melodic sound coming from one of the branches. I explored more and found that wind chimes were hanging from the tree, producing beautiful music. I enjoyed a lovely moment as I sat listening to the song from the marked tree's chimes, and I snapped a picture. I felt strangely attached to these trees that had captured my attention.

Today I drove back down the same road, only to be stopped by a police officer directing traffic. Two large trucks were in the road and a few branches were scattered here and there.

My trees were gone! Kaboom! Nothing left! In my affection for these trees, I had hoped they were marked because they had been "chosen" for something special instead of being chosen for obliteration. Sometimes being chosen feels good, and sometimes it doesn't. I think of the scripture in John 15:19:

> "If you belonged to the world, it would love you as its own. As it is, you do not belong to the world, but I have chosen you out of the world. That is why the world hates you."

God has, in a sense, put a big red X on me. Through the blood of Jesus he chose me to be his daughter. He chose me to be part of his family, and to live with him and be loved by him. That feels really good. Yet when we live for God, the world doesn't understand. That sometimes doesn't feel good.

In a way, each of us is marked with a red X. God has chosen each of us; however, we must decide to choose God in order to have a relationship with him. We can't choose both God and the world. We belong to one or the other. Jesus gives a sobering lesson using the visual of a tree.

> "Likewise every good tree bears good fruit, but a bad tree bears bad fruit. A good tree cannot bear bad fruit, and a bad tree cannot bear good fruit. Every tree that does not bear good fruit is cut down and thrown into the fire." (Matthew 7:17–19)

This makes me all the more eager to guard my heart, so that it will bear good fruit.

> Keep your heart with all vigilance,
>   for from it flow the springs of life. (Proverbs 4:23 NRSV)

As long as I live, I pray that like the wind chimes in the tree, a melody from the fruits of God's Spirit can come from my life—and that it is pleasing and delightful to him. My tree with the red X may be gone, but I'd like to think that many a home can be warmed by the wood it produced. Like the wood that comes from that tree, I long to be useful in fueling a spark that ignites and warms human hearts for God. This tree was chosen for something, but I am chosen by God for something wonderful.

> For we are God's workmanship, created in Christ Jesus to do good works, which God prepared in advance for us to do. (Ephesians 2:10)

troubles and treasures of travel 51

I have come to realize that I am a homebody. And yet for years, my job has required travel. A number of years ago, my husband and I worked with a ministry in our church that served the poor throughout numerous underdeveloped countries. It was impossible to do our job without physically going to these places so we could assess the needs and get to know the people. That required travel. Now, as part of a different assignment, we work with churches in various places, helping to strengthen and train the churches and their staffs. I am humbled and grateful to be able to serve in this way, and thankful for the life experiences we have received that enable us to give back in some way. However, I still don't like to travel.

As I write this, I'm still about four hours away from Boston, just below Iceland. My computer is sliding all over my lap, as we have hit turbulence. I hope that writing will distract me more than make me sick. My palms will soon begin to sweat—they always do when I go through turbulence. I so wish I loved to travel. Alas, I do not.

There are many trials in traveling. Though I always try to be very careful, I've managed to get food poisoning in the Philippines, Mexico, India, Romania, and most recently on another trip to Eastern Europe. Food poisoning is, quite simply, horrible. When I travel, I usually can't sleep at night, and during the day I must try to prod my body out of its deep-sleep rhythm. Since our time away is often compressed into a fairly short window of time, we often meet with people from early morning until late at night in order to make the most of the visit. Travel also involves more time than the number of days spent away from home. For many years I had to arrange care for our children while we were away; now I only have to make sure the dogs are cared for. While I'm away I also have responsibilities with my home church family that must be covered. And when I return, there is always a lot of catching up to do.

Then there is the actual transit part of travel: early mornings; traffic; taking off many items of clothing while getting X-rayed; buying a five-dollar cup of coffee; sitting for hours in a tiny airplane seat. (I am quite sure that airplane seats are made for people who are under five feet tall and weigh less than ninety pounds.) Usually luggage goes with you, but that's not always the case.

I once chuckled when I saw various toiletries and articles of clothing coming across the baggage claim conveyer belt. I felt bad for the poor person whose belongings were so scattered, and wondered what happened to their luggage—that is, until I started recognizing the articles. Yes, they were mine. My suitcase had been run over by the loaders and had been utterly destroyed.

Although travel is much easier since our nest is empty, it's still hard to be away. Yesterday as I was preparing to eat dinner with friends, I got a call informing me that my newest granddaughter had been involved in an accident and was on her way via ambulance to a children's hospital. Needless to say, I ate no dinner and offered many prayers on her behalf. She had a slight brain bleed, which was very scary. (She is doing fine and came home from the hospital the next day. Thank you, God!) It is so hard to be away from family during times like these. I felt so helpless. And yet I am always comforted to know that wherever I go

I can join hands in prayer with the Christians around me—at any given time and place—and access the creator of the universe, who happens to be my Father. And that's just what I did (and do).

So why do I keep traveling? I ask myself this question and keep coming back with the same answer.

In Luke 12, Jesus tells a poignant parable about the importance of seeking God's kingdom as first priority. He tells us to be ready for his return, to care for the poor, to have faith and focus in our daily lives. He calls us to trust that God will provide what we need. As if that's not challenge enough, at the end of this parable he adds:

> "From everyone who has been given much, much will be demanded; and from the one who has been entrusted with much, much more will be asked." (Luke 12:48)

God showers blessings upon blessings on us. I think of things I have been given by God: forgiveness of my sins, a clear conscience, direction for how to live life, the power that raised Jesus from the dead living in me, countless promises, and eternal life (to name just a few). I have been given years of training in learning to understand and apply the Scriptures. I have an amazing, godly husband, and incredible children who love God wholeheartedly and are now training their children to do so as well. They are best friends to me and to each other. I have a wonderful son who grew up in an underdeveloped country. Even through challenging times, he has taught me a new way of thinking and understanding for which I am grateful and blessed. I have a loving church family and dear friends. I have a warm home, running hot water, plenty of food, and everything I need. I have been able to connect with and meet so many wonderful people, and to see the many needs that exist throughout the world. I have been given much, and deeply desire that more and more people all over the world can know these same blessings.

I'm glad I wrote this. It reminded me again why I do what I do. As I unpack my suitcase, I will remember these amazing blessings, and next month when I pack it up again I will strive to remember and be forever grateful for the spiritual treasures God has given me to carry in "my suitcase." *Bon voyage!*

the ticket 52

Micah clutched the ticket as if he would never let go. I had placed this precious blue ticket in my youngest grandson's hand  as we rode the train back home. It was our round-trip ticket to Boston. I told him he could keep it in order to remember this special day. Micah had just handed it to the conductor, who punched holes in the ticket and gave it back to him. Today my husband and I, along with our youngest daughter and her two children, boarded a train to the city in order to visit the magnificent New England Aquarium. I don't know which was more exciting—the train ride or the aquarium. Both were awe-inspiring to Micah.

Earlier this morning, Micah (who just turned two) sat up in his crib the minute he woke up and began talking to himself about his upcoming train ride. "Choo choo!" he shouted out, and then continued to talk about seeing the conductor and riding into the city of Boston. He thought we were either going to the city of Boston or to the North Pole. He discussed both.

The whole ride was filled with wonder. We heard the whistle, watched the comings and goings of people, and noticed the scenery as the train rolled down the tracks. We marveled as the conductor walked through the train punching tickets. The conductor, in our grandson's eyes, had the coolest job in the entire world.

Then after a train change we arrived at our destination. We saw sea lions, penguins, sea turtles, sharks, and myriads of underwater sea creatures. I felt, as I observed these countless creatures, the words of the apostle Paul in Romans 1:20:

> For since the creation of the world God's invisible qualities—his eternal power and divine nature—have been clearly seen, being understood from what has been made, so that men are without excuse.

As I more closely watched the intricacies of these mysteries of the deep, the scripture in Psalm 104:24–31 came to life:

> How many are your works, O LORD!
>   In wisdom you made them all;
>   the earth is full of your creatures.
> There is the sea, vast and spacious,
>   teeming with creatures beyond number—
>   living things both large and small.
> There the ships go to and fro,
>   and the leviathan, which you formed to frolic there.
> These all look to you
>   to give them their food at the proper time.
> When you give it to them,
>   they gather it up;
> when you open your hand,
>   they are satisfied with good things.
> When you hide your face,
>   they are terrified;
> when you take away their breath,
>   they die and return to the dust.
> When you send your Spirit,
>   they are created,
>   and you renew the face of the earth.
> May the glory of the LORD endure forever;
>   may the LORD rejoice in his works.

The little blue train ticket had allowed us to travel to a place where we could see a vast array of God's handiwork. I thought of an illustration about learning the Bible that I heard Bible teacher Douglas Jacoby share. I'll paraphrase what he said:

When we first come in contact with the Bible it can be like the first time we see the ocean and think, "Wow, this is amazing!" Then we begin to read the Scriptures, and it is like hearing the waves breaking and feeling the splash of the water on our skin. We then take our study of the Word even deeper, and it is like putting our feet in the water, tasting its saltiness and feeling the surge of the tide propelling us. We might then take our study deeper, and it is like riding the waves and having them crash over us. We may think we are quite familiar with the ocean (and the Scriptures), and still we have yet to discover the vast and intricate wonders that live beneath the surface. This describes what it is like to study the Bible.

This evening my daughter sent me a text that read, "Micah took a nap with his ticket; his ticket ate with us; it has not left his hand for over an hour! I think he had a special day."

She later sent this picture of him with his bedtime bottle. His blue ticket was still tightly clutched in his little hand.

I pray that my eagerness and love for the word of God (as it leads to many wonders) may always capture my heart just as the blue train ticket (which led to many wonders) captured the heart of my grandson.

an elephant in the living room   53

The other day I was visiting a friend in Burlington, Vermont, when I noticed a small dragon walking around her living room. Trying to mask my alarm, I inquired as to the friendliness of this creature, and whether or not it was supposed to be in the living room. She told me that it was actually sunning itself, so yes—it was supposed to be there. Relieved, I tried to relax in the presence of this bizarre creature, and tried to find enjoyment in the pure delight it seemed to experience while basking in the sunlight.

This made me think: Critters of a different sort can often make their way into our living rooms and wreak havoc, while we ignore them, tiptoe around them, or pretend they are not there.

I am speaking of the proverbial "elephant in the living room." This is an expression that applies to an obvious problem that no one wants to discuss. Just as an elephant in a room would be impossible to overlook, so some issues cannot be ignored. If people in the room pretend the issue—or elephant—is not there, they have chosen to avoid dealing with reality.

Most of us have had elephants tiptoe into our living rooms at one time or another. There may even be one currently residing there.

While I think elephants are amazing creatures, I don't want one in my living room. Even so, at times I have allowed them to be there because of my fear of speaking honestly. Several scriptures have helped me. I refer to them as my "elephant busters." Here they are, with the most applicable parts emphasized:

> **Instead, speaking the truth in love,** we will in all things grow up into him who is the Head, that is, Christ. From him the whole body, joined and held together by every supporting ligament, grows and builds itself up in love, as each part does its work. (Ephesians 4:15–16)

> To the Jews who had believed him, Jesus said, "If you hold to my teaching, you are really my disciples. Then you will know the truth, and **the truth will set you free.**" (John 8:31–32)

> They came to him and said, "Teacher, we know you are a man of integrity. **You aren't swayed by men, because you pay no attention to who they are; but you teach the way of God in accordance with the truth.** Is it right to pay taxes to Caesar or not?" (Mark 12:14)

> **There is no fear in love. But perfect love drives out fear,** because fear has to do with punishment. The one who fears is not made perfect in love. (1 John 4:18)

No matter how difficult it may be, I pray to always be honest and to not let "creatures" take up residence in my living room or in any rooms of my heart.

If they move in and we ignore them, they will destroy our living rooms and leave our house full of elephant D.U.N.G. In order to avoid the refuse, there are several keys we must be aware of: Discernment, Understanding, Niceness, and Graciousness.

While speaking honestly, it is important to discern the best ways, including the best timing, to approach a difficult situation. It is also important to understand that there may be pieces missing in our understanding of the situation. A tone of gentleness and kindness (or niceness) is also something God instructs us to practice. It is also of utmost important to remember that God is a God of grace and mercy. While just, he is also merciful. He is perfectly grace and truth.

I desperately need his wisdom, power, and guidance as I go through life. May we all find the integrity, unity, freedom, and love that truth produces as we work to keep all elephants out of our living rooms.

heart monitor 54

Accessorizing is not always easy for me—especially today. For several years I have had occasional heart palpitations that have become rather annoying. So during my annual physical exam, my doctor prescribed a heart monitor in order to find out what was actually going on with my heart. Everything is probably fine, but if something needs to be treated, my doctor would like to know (as would I). After my doctor described the monitor, I envisioned a tiny little bracelet with a small button that could be pushed whenever an "event" happened. Little did I know that I would receive a semi-monstrosity (when it comes to accessories) that has wires attached to my body, and which I must wear for a month, 24/7.

And so I'm experimenting with creative ways to work this instrument into a scarf, a handbag, a giant necklace, or even a belt ornament (though I'm running short on ideas). I can only imagine what is going to happen the next time I go to the airport while wired up to my monitor—but that's another chapter.

At this point, I am always aware of my monitor's presence. It works by sending a recording of my heartbeats via satellite to someone somewhere who monitors my heart's activity. Yes, the corresponding analogies are numerous.

At times I can forget or become oblivious to the fact that God is always monitoring my heart. He is eager to point out irregularities, because he wants me spiritually healthy and strong. It can be either a comforting or a frightening thought to know that God is always monitoring our hearts, recording their thoughts and intentions. Whenever I have an "event" a buzzer goes off—and it is not quiet. Can you imagine what it would be like if we started beeping any time we had a spiritual heart "event"?

> "And you, my son Solomon, acknowledge the God of your father, and serve him with wholehearted devotion and with a willing mind, for the LORD searches every heart and understands every motive behind the thoughts. If you seek him, he will be found by you; but if you forsake him, he will reject you forever." (1 Chronicles 28:9)

> The lamp of the LORD searches the spirit of a man; it searches out his inmost being. (Proverbs 20:27)

> And he who searches our hearts knows the mind of the Spirit, because the Spirit intercedes for the saints in accordance with God's will. (Romans 8:27)

> "For the eyes of the LORD range throughout the earth to strengthen those whose hearts are fully committed to him." (2 Chronicles 16:9)

When our hearts belong to God and we seek him wholeheartedly, it is a comfort to know that he sees our hearts and can strengthen them. It's also comforting to know that God will continually cleanse us as we walk in the light (1 John 1:5–7). And yet if we are not fully committed to him and still walk in darkness, it is a frightening thought to realize that God sees our hearts. Meanwhile, our hearts will become more and more damaged, rather than healed.

As I go through the day with my new accessory, it helps me remember four areas crucial to monitoring the inside of our hearts spiritually.

First, the word of God makes us aware of the condition of our heart.

> For the word of God is living and active. Sharper than any double-edged sword, it penetrates even to dividing soul and spirit, joints and marrow; it judges the thoughts and attitudes of the heart. (Hebrews 4:12)

Second, we must have the openness and desire to change as we become sensitive to areas of our heart that God reveals and exposes.

> Search me, O God, and know my heart;
>   test me and know my anxious thoughts.
> See if there is any offensive way in me,
>   and lead me in the way everlasting. (Psalm 139:23–24)

Third, we must care about the condition of our heart and make the effort (put on our "spiritual monitor") to guard its health.

> Above all else, guard your heart,
>   for it is the wellspring of life. (Proverbs 4:23)

And fourth, we need others in our lives (the spiritual physicians or consultants) who can help us get rid of the bad and draw out the good.

> The purposes of a man's heart are deep waters,
>   but a man of understanding draws them out.
> (Proverbs 20:5)

So really, I'm not alone in wearing a heart monitor. Our hearts are all being monitored. May they find the health and healing that God desires for us all.

Meanwhile, I'm a bit stuck on how to wear this little contraption.

getting past the *ABC*s— Annoyance, Bedlam, and Chaos 55

I've renamed our dogs. Let me introduce them: Annoyance is on the left, Bedlam is front and center, and Chaos is on the right. They tested me throughout the day yesterday, and the testing culminated this morning—at four a.m. The older dog (Blackie, a.k.a. "Jackie") usually sleeps on the floor at the foot of our bed. I suppose he wasn't feeling well, since  I was awakened to the sounds of him throwing up on my pillow—right next to my head. It would have been annoying enough just to be awakened at four a.m.—but to be awakened to the sound and smell of someone barfing near your face... ugh. Thus his new nickname: Annoyance.

We also have our puppy, Denver, who is—well—a puppy. I named him Bedlam. Next there is Brady. This week we are dog-sitting Brady, our son's dog, while our son and his family are out of town. Brady is a lovable dog, who has high energy and also really loves the water. Yesterday I had decided to let the dogs out before I left for an appointment. That's when Bedlam and Chaos took over. Brady (Chaos) headed to the creek beside our house to take a little dip, and Denver (Bedlam) went the other direction, toward a swamp. Denver thought it would be fun, instead of coming when I called, to grab hold of a large stick and run the other way toward the field where some gentlemen were playing Ultimate Frisbee during their lunch hour. Finally, both dogs returned, covered in dark mud. I was not amused. Thirty minutes later, after giving the puppy a bath and watching my husband hose down Brady, I rushed with breakneck speed and high anxiety to get to my appointment.

Annoyance, bedlam and chaos are not planned. They just happen, usually at the most inopportune times. They may be, as mine were, covered with fur. Or they may come in the form of a flat tire, a flooded basement, a baby's poopy diaper, a child's tantrum, a lost shoe, a snowstorm, or even just in the form of a bad hair day. But come they will. Bedlam breaks loose, chaos erupts, and annoyances happen in what seems the mere blink of an eye. They distract us from our purpose and plans, and tempt us with frustration, anger, and anxiety.

I've learned that I can't change or avoid most of these things—so I must decide how to respond to them. I'm constantly amazed and inspired by how Jesus dealt with annoyances, bedlam, and chaos. He remained calm and purposeful amidst it all. Look at one day in the life of Jesus:

> They went to Capernaum, and when the Sabbath came, Jesus went into the synagogue and began to teach. The people were amazed at his teaching, because he taught them as one who had authority, not as the teachers of the law. Just then a man in their synagogue who was possessed by an evil spirit cried out, "What do you want with us, Jesus of Nazareth? Have you come to destroy us? I know who you are—the Holy One of God!"
>
> "Be quiet!" said Jesus sternly. "Come out of him!" The evil spirit shook the man violently and came out of him with a shriek.
>
> The people were all so amazed that they asked each other, "What is this? A new teaching—and with authority!

> He even gives orders to evil spirits and they obey him." News about him spread quickly over the whole region of Galilee.
>
> As soon as they left the synagogue, they went with James and John to the home of Simon and Andrew. Simon's mother-in-law was in bed with a fever, and they told Jesus about her. So he went to her, took her hand and helped her up. The fever left her and she began to wait on them.
>
> That evening after sunset the people brought to Jesus all the sick and demon-possessed. The whole town gathered at the door, and Jesus healed many who had various diseases. He also drove out many demons, but he would not let the demons speak because they knew who he was.
>
> Very early in the morning, while it was still dark, Jesus got up, left the house and went off to a solitary place, where he prayed. Simon and his companions went to look for him, and when they found him, they exclaimed: "Everyone is looking for you!"
>
> Jesus replied, "Let us go somewhere else—to the nearby villages—so I can preach there also. That is why I have come." (Mark 1:21–38)

In this one day in the life of Jesus, his sermon was interrupted by a crazy man. Then his plans were changed because his friend's mother-in-law (the hostess of the house where he was visiting) was very ill. He took time to heal her. Later, many sick and demon-possessed people clamored for healing. He was offered no privacy. I stand amazed and inspired by his actions and attitudes.

Several things stand out to me as Jesus met with bedlam, chaos, and annoyances. He made time to get away to pray; he was always filled with compassion amidst the chaos, bedlam, and annoyances; his desire was always to give; and he did not let himself get distracted from his purpose of telling people how to have a relationship with God. Because of his compassion and focus, I now have the hope of heaven.

May I learn from Jesus how to get past the *ABC*s of annoyance, bedlam, and chaos, so that I can help others to have a relationship with God and one day be in heaven.

the monitor told the truth   56

I felt as though I was walking into a time warp as I entered the doctor's office. The furniture, pictures, phone, and lamps were all from the 1950s. At any given moment, I expected Opie and Aunt Bee to walk into the room accompanied by Sheriff Andy Taylor. The bathroom was tiled in pink, and behind the receptionist section of the office were a Rolodex and stacks of manila file folders. There was one very old computer. When I handed the receptionist my credit card for my copayment, I was informed that they didn't accept credit cards—only cash or check. I got nervous and almost walked away. How could I entrust my heart to a doctor who worked in an antiquated office? Yet there I was. I had received an urgent call from this cardiologist asking me to come to his office. My heart monitor (mentioned in a previous chapter) had recorded an "event" over the weekend. I was well aware of the event, as my palpitations had been extreme. The doctor was concerned with the report, and called me in.

The conversation with "Dr. Sensitivity" went like this:

> Doctor: "I got a report from the monitoring center on your heart, and you've got problems."
> Me: "What kind of problems?"
> Doctor: "The kind that kill you. You should see these reports."

That got my attention. Fortunately, he quickly followed with reassurance that my "problem" was completely fixable, and that he would get me in for the needed procedure right away. So I write this knowing that tomorrow I will go to the hospital for a catheter ablation for supra-ventricular tachycardia. Yesterday I had no idea what these terms meant. Now, I realize I will *undergo* the first thing mentioned (catheter ablation), and that I *have* the second thing (supra-ventricular tachycardia). And fortunately (although I think this cardiologist is a fine doctor), a specialist will do the procedure at a hospital. I can walk out of the 1950s and into some pretty amazing technology.

This experience has made me think about a scripture that has stood out to me for many years:

> This is what the LORD says:
>
> "Cursed is the one who trusts in man,
>   who depends on flesh for his strength
>   and whose heart turns away from the LORD.
> He will be like a bush in the wastelands;
>   he will not see prosperity when it comes.
> He will dwell in the parched places of the desert,
>   in a salt land where no one lives.
>
> "But blessed is the man who trusts in the LORD,
>   whose confidence is in him.
> He will be like a tree planted by the water
>   that sends out its roots by the stream.
> It does not fear when heat comes;
>   its leaves are always green.
> It has no worries in a year of drought
>   and never fails to bear fruit."
>
> **The heart is deceitful above all things**
>   **and beyond cure.**
>   **Who can understand it?**
>
> **"I the LORD search the heart**
>   **and examine the mind,**
> to reward a man according to his conduct,
>   according to what his deeds deserve."
> (Jeremiah 17:5–10, emphasis added)

I'd been walking around with a heart problem, and I had no idea. My heart sure fooled me. But the facts revealed by the heart monitor left no doubt. There was indeed a problem.

Likewise, our hearts can deceive us into thinking we are just fine spiritually—even when we are not. When we compare what is in our hearts (as demonstrated by the way we live and talk) to the truth as seen in God's word, we may discover that we have a problem—one that can spiritually kill us.

I think I would be quite foolish to refuse to undergo the procedure that will fix my physical heart. But several things are required from me: First, I needed to understand that there is a problem. Second, I had to gain the knowledge of how to get the problem fixed. Third, I had to schedule the procedure in which the "fixing" can take place.

In order to undergo the procedure, I must be willing to surrender to the process. For the procedure to be successful, there must be a competent doctor present, and I will need to show up in the procedure room where the process takes place. *All* of these things are needed. To leave out any one of them would mean that my heart would continue to have a problem.

This experience reminds me of my conversion—the point in time when I had my "spiritual heart" fixed.

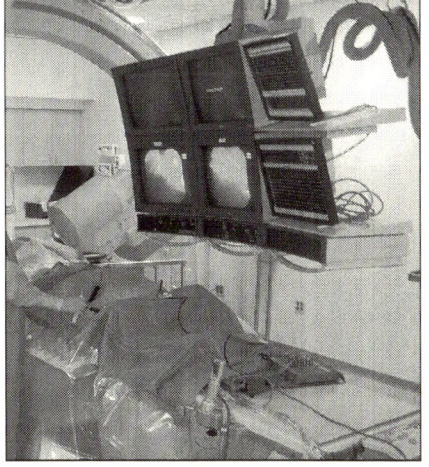

I came to understand that I had a spiritual problem, and then learned from the Bible what God said to do about it. I was willing, and surrendered to let God operate—and the Great Physician was more than capable of fixing my heart. In the procedure room of baptism, this amazing "fix"

took place. It involved God's ability and disposition to save, my surrender, and the "procedure room" of baptism where my sins were forgiven (Acts 2:38, Romans 6:3–6).

I'd be foolish to skip tomorrow's procedure, knowing that it may save my life. I'd be even more foolish if I had turned down the amazing opportunity for the spiritual healing that saved my soul.

connection correction 57

I've learned anew, in a very personal way, just how important it is to have correct connections. Earlier this week I found out that I had an extra connector, called a bypass tract, inside my heart. Two days later, I went to the hospital to get the condition corrected, as the doctors told me it was dangerous. The procedure was successful, although it was a very unpleasant experience.

There is a very specific, God-designed way, with which the human heart is meant to pump blood throughout our bodies. When an extra connector (other than the intended one) gets involved in the process, it confuses the way the heart is intended to work. The electricity can quickly jump from the correct connector to the errant connector. In my case, the electricity kept

wanting to jump the track, whenever it found my available and yet wayward connector. This resulted in a "short circuit," which is not good in an electric toaster—and perilous for a human heart.

All too often in life, we deviate from the way things were meant to be. We see before us many choices of pathways to follow. When we wander down a different path from the one God intended, numerous aspects of our lives get "short-circuited."

Whether it is the standard we use for sin and righteousness, the way we approach marriage, or even the choices we make concerning the focus of our time and attention, we can easily stray from the path of God's intended track for our lives. We may make up our own instructions, or search a different road rather than seeking out the will of God. The result can be debilitating, or even fatal—both in the present life and in the afterlife. We end up short-circuiting our souls. Although short circuits can produce fireworks for a moment and a be a "flash in the pan," they will not last. After the sparks die down, there is no more power, life, or energy.

To keep my electrical charges from straying, the doctors got rid of the errant path, or connection. I suffered true "heartburn." They literally burned the deviant connection in order to prevent it from being accessed and thus traveled again. This was a radical, but necessary, approach.

Spiritually, we can be tempted to travel superfluous or meaningless paths, different from the clear ones given by God. How much more important it is to "burn these bridges" behind us. When we eliminate those alternate paths, we are free to travel wholeheartedly down the roads our God intended.

> Acknowledge and take to heart this day that the Lord is God in heaven above and on the earth below. There is no other. (Deuteronomy 4:39)
>
> "You shall have no other gods before me."
> (Deuteronomy 5:7)
>
> So be careful to do what the Lord your God has commanded you; do not turn aside to the right or to the left. (Deuteronomy 5:32)
>
> "As for the person who hears my words but does not keep them, I do not judge him. For I did not come to judge the world, but to save it. There is a judge for the one who rejects me and does not accept my words; that very word

which I spoke will condemn him at the last day. For I did not speak of my own accord, but the Father who sent me commanded me what to say and how to say it. I know that his command leads to eternal life. So whatever I say is just what the Father has told me to say." (John 12:47–50)

"And if I go and prepare a place for you, I will come back and take you to be with me that you also may be where I am. You know the way to the place where I am going."
 Thomas said to him, "Lord, we don't know where you are going, so how can we know the way?"
 Jesus answered, "I am the way and the truth and the life. No one comes to the Father except through me." (John 14:3–6)

"Salvation is found in no one else, for there is no other name under heaven given to men by which we must be saved." (Acts 4:12)

crashing through the quitting places 58

I often take the back roads near my house in order to access the main highway. Although this path is quite curvy to navigate, the scenery is striking. My favorite corner along this route houses a pasture where a large horse can often be seen grazing. Two miniature horses are usually accompanying him. These beautiful animals always bring a smile to my face. I go a little farther and approach what the townspeople here call "death bridge." It is a narrow, rickety, one-lane bridge that spans railroad tracks below.

As I prepare to cross the bridge, my eyes always rest on a landmark that has become an eyesore to me, and likely to all who pass by. Several years ago, a garden center occupied several acres in this location. It was sold to a developer who planned to build an active retirement community. The developer displayed his plans and made a start... but never finished. Years later, this project consists of a few unfinished cement walls covered with graffiti and weeds.

For some reason, the builder did not finish what he started. I don't know what obstacles stood in the way. Perhaps he could not get the financing, or he ran into various permit restrictions. Maybe he just changed his mind. Whatever happened, this collection of cement, graffiti, and weeds is now only a monument to what could have been. It reminds me of the scripture describing the cost of following Jesus in Luke 14:28–30:

> "Suppose one of you wants to build a tower. Will he not first sit down and estimate the cost to see if he has enough money to complete it? For if he lays the foundation and is not able to finish it, everyone who sees it will ridicule him, saying, 'This fellow began to build and was not able to finish.'"

I want my life to always reflect Jesus, instead of becoming an unfinished monument of "almost, woulda, shoulda."

We are often tempted to quit before we reach breakthroughs that bring about victory or completion. Perseverance is hard. We don't even experience perseverance until we want to quit!

When are you tempted to quit? Perhaps it is when trying to overcome a character weakness or sin; or perhaps it is when beginning a new, good habit. Maybe you know that you need to find God, and yet find excuses that keep you from following through. You may need to resolve a relationship that seems too hard, or begin one that seems overwhelming. Do you have a dream you want to pursue, but have a thousand reasons why it won't work?

Through the years I have come to trust that God is capable of empowering me to do whatever he asks of me. Yet there are times when I tire of pushing through difficulties or welcoming new spiritual growth. Sometimes I get weary of simple, mundane tasks like dishes, laundry, and flossing my teeth. Then I think of scriptures such as Hebrews 10:35–39:

> So do not throw away your confidence; it will be richly rewarded. You need to persevere so that when you have done the will of God, you will receive what he has promised. For in just a very little while,
>
> "He who is coming will come and will not delay.
> But my righteous one will live by faith.

> And if he shrinks back,
>   I will not be pleased with him."
>
> But we are not of those who shrink back and are destroyed, but of those who believe and are saved.

These words help me to crash through the quitting places in my life. And I still hope that one day, as I pass by that ugly concrete slab on the way to the highway, the weeds will be gone and the foundation that was started will be a vibrant and active community, another garden center, or even a pasture where a few more horses can feed. It's not too late.

seven habits for building a strong marriage   59

Since Wyndham and I are away teaching at a marriage retreat, this seems like a good time to pen some habits my husband and I have developed over the years that have helped to make our marriage strong. Thirty-seven years later, there is no one I would rather spend time with than my husband—my best friend.

If I were to list the most important habits we have incorporated into our marriage, they would be:

1. Practice daily prayer together. It has been so meaningful to us to take our gratitude, concerns, and requests to God as a couple, as well as individually. I love the scripture in Exodus 33:12–17:

> Moses said to the LORD, "You have been telling me, 'Lead these people,' but you have not let me know whom you will send with me. You have said, 'I know you by name and you have found favor with me.' If you are pleased with me, teach me your ways so I may know you and continue to find favor with you. Remember that this nation is your people."

> The LORD replied, "My Presence will go with you, and I will give you rest."
> Then Moses said to him, "If your Presence does not go with us, do not send us up from here. How will anyone know that you are pleased with me and with your people unless you go with us? What else will distinguish me and your people from all the other people on the face of the earth?"
> And the LORD said to Moses, "I will do the very thing you have asked, because I am pleased with you and I know you by name."

Our marriage is strong because we have chosen to practice his Presence with us. Having God with us in our marriage means everything. We cannot guide it or carry it alone. We always need his Presence and involvement in our marriage.

2. Have a purposeful assessment and planning time together each week.

We have found that life gets away from us if we don't deliberately make plans along with our prayers.

Every week we take some extended time together to talk about our spiritual and emotional state of being, what is going on in our lives, as well as well as what areas need growth. We follow this with some extended prayer time together.

> Therefore, prepare your minds for action; be self-controlled; set your hope fully on the grace to be given you when Jesus Christ is revealed. As obedient children, do not conform to the evil desires you had when you lived in ignorance. But just as he who called you is holy, so be holy in all you do; for it is written: "Be holy, because I am holy."
> (1 Peter 1:13–16)

If we don't set aside a time to plan and prepare our minds for action, things get crazy and we end up not living out our priorities in our day-to-day schedules.

Our "bumps" have usually come from unmet or differing expectations, resulting from issues that we did not talk through together ahead of time.

When our children were still at home, we also talked through their schedules—considering their physical and emotional needs, how we would prioritize getting time with them, and how we would include time for family devotionals. We strove to have a deliberate approach for developing the spiritual and emotional connections in our family, seeking feedback from within and without the family.

3. Eat together at the dinner table. Most days (with a rare exception) we strove to have everyone together at the family dinner table. These were precious times. We still enjoy dinner together, even as empty nesters. It has also served us well to go to bed at the same time most nights.

4. Practice openness and transparency. We have found it extremely beneficial to consistently have another couple or two in our lives who know us really well and care about our spiritual, emotional, and physical wellbeing. We open up our lives to them. This practice not only helps us grow, but it also helps us get rid of blind spots that can weigh us down. These friends provide a place to get "unstuck" if we come to an impasse.

5. Cultivate a lifestyle focused on other people.

> Devote yourselves to prayer, being watchful and thankful. And pray for us, too, that God may open a door for our message, so that we may proclaim the mystery of Christ, for which I am in chains. Pray that I may proclaim it clearly, as I should. Be wise in the way you act toward outsiders; make the most of every opportunity. Let your conversation be always full of grace, seasoned with salt, so that you may know how to answer everyone. (Colossians 4:2–6)

> All they asked was that we should continue to remember the poor, the very thing I was eager to do. (Galatians 2:10)

Practicing hospitality in our home, along with finding ways to serve the poor, has served our marriage and family in a tremendous way. It truly is more blessed to give than to receive, and these practices have reminded us and our children that we are not the center of the universe, but are instead meant to give, and to serve others. This habit has refreshed our souls over and over again.

6. Express love and affection to each other daily—don't just assume they're a "given." I'm amazed at the ways God expresses his love for me in the Scriptures, through people, and through his creation. My husband consistently encourages me and expresses his affection toward me. This practice helps me (and our family) remember why we love each other, and encourages us to keep on giving.

7. Enjoy God's pleasant boundaries.

> The boundary lines have fallen for me in pleasant places; surely I have a delightful inheritance. (Psalm 16:6)

It's so important to enjoy each other, and to enjoy the pleasant boundaries we have been given. That's why you may find us taking a walk, sipping coffee on the front porch as the sun sets, sitting by the fire, riding our bicycles, walking in the snow, playing with our grandchildren, running our dogs, licking a frozen yogurt cone at Bedford Farms, hiking a trail, or watching the waves roll on the North Shore.

It's never too late to begin good habits!

falling into holes 60

I fell into a hole today. Other than the humiliation of being sprawled out on the lawn of a funeral home, and the inconvenience of a sprained, swollen, and black-and-blue pinky finger, there were no serious repercussions. Sometimes I feel like holes in the ground just wait for me—or perhaps I'm just a bit of a klutz.

One of my most memorable falls happened a number of years ago in my backyard. We had unsuccessfully tried to breed our long-haired dachshund, Brandy, to a dapper young male 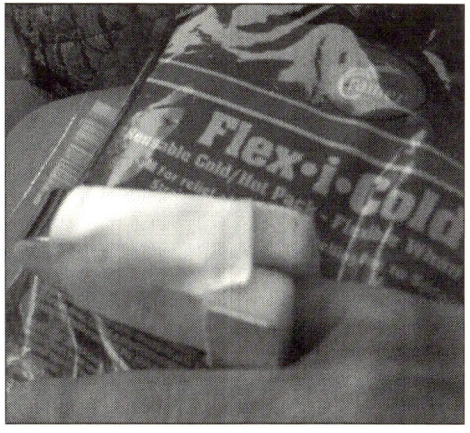 dachshund. Brandy wanted nothing to do with him. Her heart belonged to the poodle down the street. Soon after we ended the unsuccessful visit with the young dachshund suitor, I looked outside my kitchen window to discover that the neighbor's poodle had come calling. He had climbed our chain link fence to "wed" our little dachshund. I instinctively grabbed a broom and ran out of the house to chase the poodle—whose heart's desire was obviously bent on fathering Brandy's first puppies. As I was racing around the yard chasing the poodle with the broom, I fell facedown into a hole. Alas, I was unable to sweep away the suitor, who was already quite "swept away." I feel confident that if this awkward scene had been captured in the YouTube era, it would have gone viral. Alas, this fall had consequences—scraped arms and knees and six long, grey, curly-haired, adorable dach-a-poos.

Falling into holes can hurt, and leave all kinds of lingering physical consequences. However, there are also "spiritual holes" we can trip over or fall into. The results can be far more devastating. These holes can be little pits of distraction, or gaping craters of anxiety and worry. We can be sure that all forces of evil will try to dig holes around us, hoping to trip us up.

As I read the scriptures below, I was struck by the charge from God to make level paths for my feet. How can I make my ground level?

I can do this by learning from God's discipline and throwing off the things that hinder me or trip me up, and by fixing my eyes on Jesus.

> Therefore, since we are surrounded by such a great cloud of witnesses, let us throw off everything that hinders and the sin that so easily entangles, and let us run with perseverance the race marked out for us. Let us fix our eyes on Jesus, the author and perfecter of our faith, who for the joy set before him endured the cross, scorning its shame, and sat down at the right hand of the throne of God. Consider him who endured such opposition from sinful men, so that you will not grow weary and lose heart....
>
> And you have forgotten that word of encouragement that addresses you as sons:
>
> "My son, do not make light of the Lord's discipline,
> and do not lose heart when he rebukes you..."
>
> Therefore, strengthen your feeble arms and weak knees. "Make level paths for your feet," so that the lame may not be disabled, but rather healed. (Hebrews 12:1–3, 5, 12–13)

I deeply appreciate that even though I may be clumsy on my feet, I have a God who is willing to hold me up and keep me steady.

To him who is able to keep you from falling and to present you before his glorious presence without fault and with great joy—to the only God our Savior be glory, majesty, power and authority, through Jesus Christ our Lord, before all ages, now and forevermore! Amen. (Jude 24–25)

dinner with a friend 61

Whenever time and finances allow, there are few things I enjoy more than eating dinner with friends. Last night, I experienced dining at its finest! I had a free meal with a special friend. We ate cereal, cookies, cupcakes, ice cream, pasta, and soup. The nonstop conversation was meaningful, and at the end of the meal our bellies were full. I tried several times to stand to stretch my legs or to go in and join the grown-ups in the other room—only  to be instructed to sit back down in order to talk and eat a little longer.

Fortunately, I used no Weight Watchers points during this meal. The food was imaginary, and my grandson-friend is two years old. It was just the two of us, conversing and enjoying each other's company. This special meal brought to life a scripture I read today in Revelation 3:14–20:

> "To the angel of the church in Laodicea write:
> These are the words of the Amen, the faithful and true witness, the ruler of God's creation. I know your deeds, that you are neither cold nor hot. I wish you were either one or the other! So, because you are lukewarm—neither hot nor cold—I am about to spit you out of my mouth. You

say, 'I am rich; I have acquired wealth and do not need a thing.' But you do not realize that you are wretched, pitiful, poor, blind and naked. I counsel you to buy from me gold refined in the fire, so you can become rich; and white clothes to wear, so you can cover your shameful nakedness; and salve to put on your eyes, so you can see.

Those whom I love I rebuke and discipline. So be earnest, and repent. Here I am! I stand at the door and knock. If anyone hears my voice and opens the door, I will come in and eat with him, and he with me."

This passage of scripture (especially verses 20, 21) is often misused, especially when read out of context. These verses were never intended to instruct one on how to become a Christian. These words were written to a church in Laodicea (an ancient Roman province of Asia). Since this letter was addressed to a church, the recipients of this letter were individuals who had already become Christians. These verses, however, do relay a most amazing message!

The Christians in Laodicea, who had at one time had made Jesus the Lord of their lives, had now become complacent and lukewarm. Although they were in an unacceptable state before God, they still felt pretty good about themselves. They had forgotten their absolute dependence on and need for their Lord.

Jesus, through his strong words, attempts to stir their hearts to awaken them spiritually so that they will change their course. I try to picture this scene, where the group is gathered together as a church and Jesus is banging at the door saying, "I'm here! Let me in!"

What amazes me is Jesus' desire to sit at our table—to sit and talk and dine with us. (And these verses were written after Jesus had been treated with apathy and contempt.) If I try to walk away, it's as if he has the same desire that my grandson expressed: "Sit, stay, don't leave. Let's keep talking and eating."

My grandson wanted to share a "meal" with me. He was looking for my devotion and attention (my heart). He was actually better at this dining experience than I was. He was not distracted by "more important" things. I'm touched that my grandson wanted to sit and eat with me.

I'm more in awe that my Creator wants to come and "eat with me." I know he is looking for my devotion, my attention—my heart; yet I can too often become distracted with other things vying for my attention. I know nothing is more important than his presence in my life. Why should I ever want (through complacency, distraction, or apathy) to leave a meal with Jesus? He provides the menu that truly fills me, and the ambiance that brings me peace and security.

Are you enjoying his presence at your table, or is he banging at your door?

the day I was born   62

Fifty-eight years ago today, Porter Horne's mother was exceedingly grateful. The Hornes, a family with two little boys, lived across the pond from my family's house. On this particular day, March 23, 1954, five-year-old Porter was enjoying a tricycle ride with his older brother—until something went terribly wrong. Porter rode his little trike down the dock and never put on the brakes. He and his tricycle fell into the water. His frightened brother ran to get their mother. Their panicked mother, who could not swim, noticed my dad's car pulling into his driveway at that exact time. She screamed to my dad that her son was at the bottom of the pond. My dad ran to the pond, jumped in, and pulled the lifeless boy out of the murky water. After a few minutes of mouth-to-mouth resuscitation, the boy began to breathe. An ambulance arrived to take him to the local hospital, where he completely recovered.

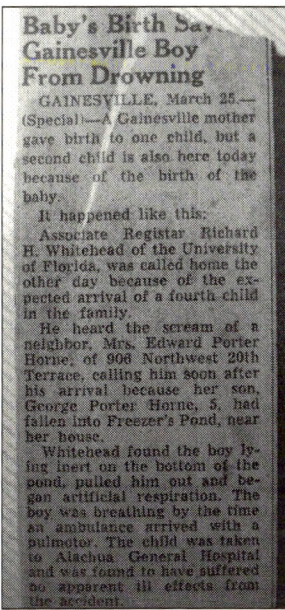

The headline from the *Tampa Tribune* the next day read, "Baby's Birth Saves Gainesville Boy from Drowning." You see, my mother had called my dad home that particular morning because she was in labor with me. It happened at just the right time and place... not a minute too soon or too late.

I don't remember anything about the day I was born, but I'm sure Mrs. Horne remembered. And I'm sure my parents remembered. What is even more special to me is that God remembers, and knows the day I was born.

> For you created my inmost being;
>   you knit me together in my mother's womb.
> I praise you because I am fearfully and wonderfully made;
>   your works are wonderful,
>   I know that full well.
> My frame was not hidden from you
>   when I was made in the secret place.
> When I was woven together in the depths of the earth,
>   your eyes saw my unformed body.
> All the days ordained for me
>   were written in your book
>   before one of them came to be. (Psalm 139:13–16)

These verses amaze me, showing me that I'm known, created, and cared for by God.

> "From one man he made every nation of men that they should inhabit the whole earth; and he determined the times set for them and the exact places where they should live. God did this so that men would seek him and perhaps reach out for him and find him, though he is not far from each one of us." (Acts 17:26–27)

I am humbled that God also picked the time and place for me to live in order for me to seek him, reach out for him, and find him. I am also truly amazed that God looks at each of us as described in the scripture below. Regardless of the circumstances to which we were born and whether or not any person cares that we were born, *God* cares. He wants us to feel valued and known; to seek him and be found by him.

I have had the incredible privilege of knowing and loving many people who grew up as orphans and never knew the date of their birth. After some research, I was able to celebrate birthdays with many of them for the first time. Their life had previously not been celebrated by another person. But God had been celebrating them all along.

> The word of the LORD came to me: "Son of man, confront Jerusalem with her detestable practices and say, 'This is what the Sovereign LORD says to Jerusalem: Your ancestry and birth were in the land of the Canaanites; your father was an Amorite and your mother a Hittite. On the day you were born your cord was not cut, nor were you washed with water to make you clean, nor were you rubbed with salt or wrapped in cloths. No one looked on you with pity or had compassion enough to do any of these things for you. Rather, you were thrown out into the open field, for on the day you were born you were despised.
>
> "'Then I passed by and saw you kicking about in your blood, and as you lay there in your blood I said to you, "Live!" I made you grow like a plant of the field.'"
> (Ezekiel 16:1–7)

I particularly miss my mom and dad on my birthday, as I think about the difference they made in my life from that day forward—as well as the difference they made in Porter Horne's life, his parents' lives, his brother's life, and so many, many other lives. I pray that my life can also be used to help other people find life.

getting "unstuck" 63

Denver, our golden retriever pup, had me worried yesterday. He was sick to his stomach and lethargic throughout the day and evening. Even as all the kids and grandkids gathered for a family dinner last night, Denver didn't want to play—and he always wants to play! Clearly, something wasn't right. His demeanor reminded me of a time when his half-brother (my daughter Kristen's dog, Luke) was ill and needed surgery in order to survive. It was a rough time, and many prayers and dollars later, a turquoise pacifier emerged from the dog's intestines into the surgeon's hands. The "stuck" object had to be removed in order for him to survive. As long as it was lodged in his intestines, he could not take in any food or nutrients for processing. Fortunately, he got "unstuck." Luke is now an active, healthy, three-year-old dog.

This morning during his walk, Denver got his strength back. He got unstuck. Just when it seemed he was heading for a trip to the vet, a surprise appeared. Yes, here it is (hosed off for pictures) in all its glory. Denver had eaten (in its entirety) a stuffed mouse—red with little green ears and beady eyes. I don't know where he found it, but I was certainly grateful that the mouse made it through to the other side. Otherwise, the consequences could have been dire.

How often we can take things in to our hearts and minds and

get "stuck" because we don't have an outlet for them. We can become like the Dead Sea. The Dead Sea does not support life because it has no outward flow.

The Samaritan woman in John 4 provides an example of one who was stuck in her fear, hopelessness, and sin—until she met Jesus. He offered her a path to courage, hope, and forgiveness.

> When a Samaritan woman came to draw water, Jesus said to her, "Will you give me a drink?" (His disciples had gone into the town to buy food.)
> The Samaritan woman said to him, "You are a Jew and I am a Samaritan woman. How can you ask me for a drink?" (For Jews do not associate with Samaritans.)
> Jesus answered her, "If you knew the gift of God and who it is that asks you for a drink, you would have asked him and he would have given you living water."
> "Sir," the woman said, "you have nothing to draw with and the well is deep. Where can you get this living water? Are you greater than our father Jacob, who gave us the well and drank from it himself, as did also his sons and his flocks and herds?"
> Jesus answered, "Everyone who drinks this water will be thirsty again, but whoever drinks the water I give him will never thirst. Indeed, the water I give him will become in him a spring of water welling up to eternal life."
> The woman said to him, "Sir, give me this water so that I won't get thirsty and have to keep coming here to draw water." (John 4:7–15)

Whenever I am stuck because of fear, discouragement, or lack of faith, I must then realize I have choices before me. I can hold these things inside and try to carry them myself. When I do this, it does not free me or help me get unstuck. Instead, like the ingested stuffed mouse, I just become stagnant and stinky.

Or I can choose to take these things to Jesus. He, through the living water he gives me, gets me unstuck. When I get unstuck, then I can pass on the effects of this living water to people around me. I need and count on this great promise.

> For the Lamb at the center of the throne will be their
>   shepherd;
>   he will lead them to springs of living water.
> And God will wipe away every tear from their eyes.
> (Revelation 7:17)

can a truck say "choo choo"? 64

My two-year-old grandchildren had a discussion this morning. My daughter summed up the context of their debate for me. Lexi was trying to convince Micah that trucks could say "choo choo." Micah disagreed, insisting that only trains could say "choo choo." According to Micah, that sound was not for trucks, but was reserved for trains. After some friendly bantering,  they both agreed to disagree, and moved on to their next game of taking pretend naps on the floor.

So can a truck say "choo choo"? I suppose so, but personally, I think "choo choo" would be better said by the train. A truck is not really meant to say "choo choo." It has other noises it needs to make, such as "vroom vroom."

As I thought about their conversation, I thought about the differences between the train and the truck. I considered how we are each created with different strengths. I'm often struck by how similar but unique we all are. We each have specific ways in which we can use our particular gifts.

I love God's church and the way he puts all her parts together. Like an orchestra, when each part is doing what it does best and is working together, the resulting harmony is stunning. Everyone is important, everyone is needed. Our differences teach us how to honor one another. We are not meant to function as a "church of one." God has put us together for a reason. We need each other. God planned and designed us to function together as a body, a family, a household—his church. We are meant to love each other and belong to each other.

> Therefore, I urge you, brothers, in view of God's mercy, to offer your bodies as living sacrifices, holy and pleasing to God—this is your spiritual act of worship....
>
> For by the grace given me I say to every one of you: Do not think of yourself more highly than you ought, but rather think of yourself with sober judgment, in accordance with the measure of faith God has given you. Just as each of us has one body with many members, and these members do not all have the same function, so in Christ we who are many form one body, and each member belongs to all the others. We have different gifts, according to the grace given us. If a man's gift is prophesying, let him use it in proportion to his faith. If it is serving, let him serve; if it is teaching, let him teach; if it is encouraging, let him encourage; if it is contributing to the needs of others, let him give generously; if it is leadership, let him govern diligently; if it is showing mercy, let him do it cheerfully.
>
> Love must be sincere. Hate what is evil; cling to what is good. Be devoted to one another in brotherly love. Honor one another above yourselves. (Romans 12:1, 3–10)

Today I am so grateful for the ways I see people in the church devote themselves and offer themselves to God's service and to one another. Like the truck, I will likely do best when I "vroom vroom" rather than "choo choo." However, I desperately need the "choo choos" surrounding me. We all need each other's uniqueness as we are united in conviction and purpose. May we each wholeheartedly offer ourselves—and what we uniquely contribute to God's church.

showing up　　　　　　　　　　　65

Before I retire for the night, I let both dogs go outside. It's my routine every evening. They do their business and are always eager to come back inside for their nighttime treats. Last night was meant to be no different. The dogs went out. The puppy came bounding back, eager to do all of his new tricks and eat his doggie treat. Blackie (a.k.a. "Jackie") didn't return.

It was raining outside, so I reasoned that he must have needed a little more time. However, I thought that he should have been very eager to come in to the warm, dry house. After a few minutes I called him again. No response. The next day was trash collection day, so I surmised that he was sniffing out a few garbage cans. Thirty minutes went by—still no response. Then my imagination kicked in. I pictured him in the mouth of a coyote, cornered by angry skunks, stuck in a fence, or even sleeping beside a pot-bellied pig at a neighbor's house. (That actually happened with a dog we previously owned!)

As it neared midnight, I was faced with a conundrum. Should I go searching, or just wait for his return? I scoped out the usual places and loudly called his name (sorry, neighbors)—but still no

Blackie. I knew I would need sleep to prepare for a busy day, so I crawled into bed, but I couldn't sleep. What if he was hurt, lost, or in trouble? I prayed, and then watched shows on the Food Network. I checked

the front door at every commercial. As I went to the door time and time again, I saw nothing.

Yes, nothing! It was such a sad, disappointing sight. I kept envisioning the fluffy little ball of fur at my door, but seeing nothing. One a.m.—nothing. One-thirty a.m.—nothing. Two a.m.—nothing.

I got to thinking about how God feels when he waits for me to "show up" with him each morning. I can get busy or distracted and miss needed time spent with him in prayer and the Scriptures. I can at times take time with God for granted, and exchange what is important for what feels urgent. Perhaps one of the most convicting, piercing scriptures to me is from Luke 10:38–42:

> As Jesus and his disciples were on their way, he came to a village where a woman named Martha opened her home to him. She had a sister called Mary, who sat at the Lord's feet listening to what he said. But Martha was distracted by all the preparations that had to be made. She came to him and asked, "Lord, don't you care that my sister has left me to do the work by myself? Tell her to help me!"
>
> "Martha, Martha," the Lord answered, "you are worried and upset about many things, but only one thing is needed. Mary has chosen what is better, and it will not be taken away from her."

I recently read an article from Robert Boyd Munger's "*My Heart Christ's Home.*" The following paragraphs moved me deeply as the author described a conversation with Jesus as he visited different rooms of our heart.

> We walked next into the drawing room. This room was rather intimate and comfortable. I liked it. It had a fireplace, overstuffed chairs, a bookcase, sofa, and a quiet atmosphere.
>
> He [Jesus] also seemed pleased with it. He said, "This is indeed a delightful room. Let us come here often. It is se-

cluded and quiet and we can have fellowship together...."
He promised, "I will be here every morning early. Meet with me here and we will start the day together." So, morning after morning, I would come downstairs into the drawing room and He would take a book of the Bible... open it and we would read together. He would tell me of its riches and unfold to me its truths... They were wonderful hours together... But little by little, under the pressure of many responsibilities, this time began to be shortened.... I began to miss a day now and then.... I would miss it two days in a row and often more.

I remember one day when I was in a hurry... As I passed the drawing room, the door was ajar. Looking in I saw a fire in the fireplace and the Lord sitting there.... " Blessed Master, forgive me. Have you been here all these mornings?"

"Yes," He said. "I told you I would be here every morning to meet with you." Then I was even more ashamed. He had been faithful in spite of my faithlessness. I asked His forgiveness and He readily forgave me...

He said, "The trouble with you is this: You have been thinking of the quiet time, of the Bible study and prayer time, as a factor in your own spiritual progress, but you have forgotten that this hour means something to Me also."[1]

Last night, I finally fell asleep for a couple of hours. When I awoke at four-thirty a.m., I checked the door again. Blackie was there at the door, soaking wet and acting as if nothing had happened. I was finally able to fall sound asleep. He was home, out of harm's way.

It is a great privilege to spend time with God, and I know how deeply I need it. Often, just showing up is the hardest part. Not only do I become very vulnerable when I don't show up, but I can fail to see that this time matters to him.

---

1. Robert Boyd Munger, *My Heart—Christ's Home* (Downers Grove, IL: InterVarsity Press, 1986)

walking the power lines 66

I love prayer walks. Wyndham and I often walk along a gravel path near our house that follows several miles of power lines. Yesterday as we walked and prayed (and scolded Denver for eating the leash), I kept noticing the path of wires above me.

While it is sometimes disconcerting to hear the electricity's snap, crackle, and pop in these wires while we walk, I also marvel at the power traveling through them. I've also wondered (since I have actually been hit by lightning, and often walk under power lines) if I am overcharged with electrical current. (Is it just me, or do other people often get shocked when touching food on grocery shelves?) Regardless, it is perplexing to me to ponder the way that power in these wires accomplishes so much.

I try to imagine what goes on inside of those wires—knowing that at any given moment the flick of a switch allows me to turn darkness to light in my kitchen. Miles away, someone else can stay warm even when the temperature outside is frigid—all because of the power going through these wires.

Even more amazing is what goes on in heaven as I walk under these wires. I can open my mouth or just speak from my heart, and the Creator of the universe who gave me the breath of life not only hears what I say, but is able to act on it. While it's incredible to look up and realize that the power going through the wires enables me to see when it is dark and also allows someone else miles away to stay warm when it's freezing outside—this pales in comparison to what goes on in the spiritual realm beyond the wires.

Because of the prayers we pray as we walk the power lines (or anywhere we may be), astounding things can happen. When I focus my prayers on specific individuals, situations, and churches—whether here at home or across the ocean—I don't know all that is happening in the spiritual realm, but I do know that power is being directed. While I don't know how God will answer my prayers, I have seen inexplicable answers to these prayers.

As I read my Bible, I recount times when directed prayer resulted in a nation crossing an ocean on dry ground; a giant falling because of a shepherd boy's slingshot; a man staying safe while in a den of lions; and three men walking in an inferno without a single hair on their bodies being singed. After prayer, thousands were fed from two fish and five loaves of bread, jail doors miraculously opened... and on and on I could go with examples.

> I will remember the deeds of the LORD;
>   yes, I will remember your miracles of long ago.
> I will meditate on all your works
>   and consider all your mighty deeds.
>
> Your ways, O God, are holy.
>   What god is so great as our God?
> You are the God who performs miracles;
>   you display your power among the peoples.
> With your mighty arm you redeemed your people,
>   the descendants of Jacob and Joseph.
>
> The waters saw you, O God,
>   the waters saw you and writhed;
>   the very depths were convulsed.
> The clouds poured down water,
>   the skies resounded with thunder;

> your arrows flashed back and forth.
> Your thunder was heard in the whirlwind,
> > your lightning lit up the world;
> > the earth trembled and quaked.
> Your path led through the sea,
> > your way through the mighty waters,
> > though your footprints were not seen. (Psalm 77:11–19)

Most days I meet people who hold to a form of religion. But as I speak to them, I learn that all too often this form of religion lacks power to change their lives; to make them feel secure and complete; to be confident about their eternity; to overcome sin; to build strong marriages; to give and receive forgiveness; and to build relationships that help them be more like Jesus.

> People will be lovers of themselves, lovers of money, boastful, proud, abusive, disobedient to their parents, ungrateful, unholy, without love, unforgiving, slanderous, without self-control, brutal, not lovers of the good, treacherous, rash, conceited, lovers of pleasure rather than lovers of God—**having a form of godliness but denying its power.** (2 Timothy 3:2–5, emphasis added)

As I walk along the power lines, I am reminded that God's power was made available to me through Jesus' death, burial, and resurrection.

> I am not ashamed of the gospel, because it is the power of God for the salvation of everyone who believes: first for the Jew, then for the Gentile. (Romans 1:16)

The power available to me in my life is the same power that raised Jesus from the dead (Romans 8:11); is made perfect in my weakness (2 Corinthians 12:9); can accomplish more than I dare ask or imagine (Ephesians 3:20, 21); and gives me everything I need for life and godliness (2 Peter 1:3).

My connection to God accesses power that is beyond anything physical or within the dimensions of my understanding. So as I walk along the power lines, I pray to always be humbled by the power of God and never forget or fail to claim the power available to me through my relationship with God.

were cows just here? 67

Did a herd of cows visit my yard last night?

My olfactory senses were awakened as I walked outside my door this morning. The smell of manure was intense. I had noticed this same smell at the town office where I had just run an errand. It seemed that the herd had visited the town office yard as well. Upon inquiring, I learned that all town-owned properties had received a generous dump of manure-based fertilizer. Since our house is surrounded by a town park, we were beneficiaries of this very special aroma. Even as I write, the smell of cow dung is filling my nostrils. It's not pleasant.

There are many things I love to smell. I love the smell of bread baking, or of cookies in the oven. My mouth waters when I come inside my house to the smell of a roast, especially when it is cooking with onions and garlic. I enjoy the smell of coffee brewing in the morning. I will soon enjoy the fragrance of lilacs in my back yard. There are things I don't like to smell, and the concoction spread on the field by my house is near the top of the list.

It is interesting to me to learn that God has a keen sense of smell. Thirty-nine times, the Old Testament speaks of aromas that are pleasing to God. It speaks most often of how God enjoys the aroma of roasted lamb; it also mentions that he enjoys the smell of beef or bread being baked over a fire.

Actually, these thirty-nine verses aren't written so we can know what kind of food God prefers. Upon further study, the pleasing aroma comes not so much from the smell of the food cooking, but from the hearts of the people who laid these sacrifices on the altar. Yes, God can smell our hearts! People who were eager to sacrifice and to obey the will of God brought him great joy. He also knew when someone's sacrifice was obligatory or from leftovers. He was, and always has been, looking to see what is in our hearts as we approach him. God has shown us his love in a way that no one else ever has by giving us his only Son. In response, he desires our hearts—completely.

> Therefore, I urge you, brothers, in view of God's mercy, to offer your bodies as living sacrifices, holy and pleasing to God—this is your spiritual act of worship. (Romans 12:1)

In the New Testament, the new and superior plan God gave us after Jesus died, we find that God's sense of smell has not changed.

> But thanks be to God, who always leads us in triumphal procession in Christ and through us spreads everywhere the fragrance of the knowledge of him. For we are to God the aroma of Christ among those who are being saved and those who are perishing. To the one we are the smell of death; to the other, the fragrance of life. And who is equal to such a task? Unlike so many, we do not peddle the word of God for profit. On the contrary, in Christ we speak before God with sincerity, like men sent from God. (2 Corinthians 2:14-17)

This scripture tells me that when I walk with Jesus and spread the news of him, it smells wonderful to God. As I follow Christ I leave the fragrance of "eau de knowledge of Christ," which is the most precious of all fragrances. People whose hearts desire to know God love this fragrance and gravitate towards it. To people who don't want to change their lives to please God, the fragrance stinks.

   I pray that the best fragrance known to God can exude from me today... and I sure hope it can overcome the stench outside.

get outta my house 68

It was bedtime, so I told Denver (now five months old) to get in his crate. He looked at me as if he was afraid of something, and refused to go into his crate. Then I heard a growling noise. I could not figure out what was going on, so I began searching for clues. When I peered into his crate, I saw two beady eyes staring back at me. Blackie (the "older brother cockerpoo" who reluctantly and sporadically accepts the newbie) was stretched out on the pillow in Denver's crate, as if daring Denver to come in to his own crate.

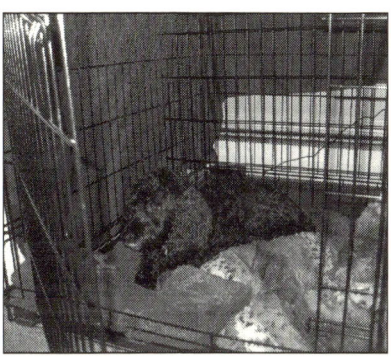

I thought to myself, "Blackie gets full reign of our house, but now he wants Denver's crate too? Who does he think he is? And Denver refuses to get into his own crate? Does Denver not realize that he now towers over Blackie?"

I laughed as I observed this unspoken canine communication. Denver had let the little "alpha dog" take what rightfully belonged to him. I looked at Blackie with disapproval, and as if he could read my mind, he slithered out of Denver's crate.

I began thinking about this little exchange between the dogs and wondered: Who do we let take over "our house"? It often seems that someone or something tries to take away what has been given to us by God. He has already given us everything we need for life and godliness.

> His divine power has given us everything we need for life and godliness through our knowledge of him who called us by his own glory and goodness. (2 Peter 1:3)

In Christ, I possess not only everything that I need, but also what every person in this world needs. Paul expressed this reality as he prayed that everyone could have what he had, and be what he had become in Christ (except for the imprisonment he experienced). He knew that the forgiveness of sins he had been given, the purpose in life he possessed, and the relationships he shared were what everyone on earth needed. This fact not only gives me confidence; it also gives me urgency to share this gift.

> Paul replied, "Short time or long—I pray God that not only you but all who are listening to me today may become what I am, except for these chains." (Acts 26:29)

Despite all I have been given, I can at times get fearful or timid in my faith. I can be like Denver, who let a small growling dog keep him from going into his own "house."

My spiritual house is filled with so many blessings and promises from God. God has promised me peace that passes understanding (Philippians 4:7). So why do I let worries of this world keep me from that peace? He has promised that he can do more than I ask or imagine (Ephesians 3:20). So why do I struggle with wondering if something is too big for God to change? He has promised that he will hear my prayers (1 John 5:15). So why do I sometimes fail to pray to him with confidence? God's word is living and active (Hebrews 4:12), so why don't I always use it to convict my own heart as well as the hearts of others? God has given me a spirit of power, love, and self-control, so why would I let any of these obstacles keep me from possessing what has been given to me?

> For God did not give us a spirit of timidity, but a spirit of power, of love and of self-discipline. (2 Timothy 1:7)

> Submit yourselves, then, to God. Resist the devil, and he will flee from you. (James 4:7)

With Jesus I am more than a conqueror. Nothing has the power to separate me from the love and power of God. Nothing has the power, no matter how loud the growl or beady the eyes, to keep me out of the spiritual house God has provided for me.

> What, then, shall we say in response to this? If God is for us, who can be against us? He who did not spare his own Son, but gave him up for us all—how will he not also, along with him, graciously give us all things? Who will bring any charge against those whom God has chosen? It is God who justifies. Who is he that condemns? Christ Jesus, who died—more than that, who was raised to life—is at the right hand of God and is also interceding for us. Who shall separate us from the love of Christ? Shall trouble or hardship or persecution or famine or nakedness or danger or sword? As it is written:
>
> "For your sake we face death all day long;
>   we are considered as sheep to be slaughtered."
>
> No, in all these things we are more than conquerors through him who loved us. For I am convinced that neither death nor life, neither angels nor demons, neither the present nor the future, nor any powers, neither height nor depth, nor anything else in all creation, will be able to separate us from the love of God that is in Christ Jesus our Lord. (Romans 8:31–39)

two important words: "help me!"   69

The drowning victim was barely able to utter the words, "Help me!"

I remembered those crucial words today as I passed by several empty lifeguard chairs. My lunch appointment had cancelled, so I joined some of my grandchildren who were picnicking with their moms at a local lake. I sat in the lifeguard chair remembering the day more than thirty-seven years ago when I was that victim calling for help.

The day before my wedding, I was scheduled to take my last finals of college. I would finally be finished with school! For fun I had taken a lifesaving course as an elective. The lifesaving certification test was one of my day-before-the-wedding exams. Unfortunately for me, we had experienced some unseasonably cool December temperatures for Florida, and the heater in the pool was not working. (This was well before the school's large indoor sports arena was built.) The pool used for swim meets and for our lifesaving class was outside. It was cold. I still remember dreading the cold as I threw off my sweat suit and dove into the water. (The water was in the sixties, which is fairly normal for the New England Atlantic, but for my Florida blood it felt frigid.)

Since the heater was broken, the woman who was scheduled to be the "drowning victim" for the girls' test didn't show up at the pool on this test day. She assumed, because of the broken heater and the cold weather, that the testing had been postponed. My classmates could reschedule their tests, but since I was getting married and moving the following day, I didn't have that option. My instructor found someone nearby who was willing to be my "victim" for the test: the University of Florida varsity men's soccer coach. I remember looking at his very muscular frame and hoping he would be kind to me as I tried to "save" him. He was not. He struggled with me, pulled me into a head hold, and began to take me under (as many victims do). I began going under, and felt my legs cramp with excruciating pain. They just wouldn't work because of the cold water.

As I gasped for air, I looked at him and screamed, "Help me!" He pulled me out—and although I never retook my test, I was happy to be alive and able to marry my wonderful husband the next day.

The simple words "help me" are sometimes hard to say, but they are extremely important. I didn't want to ask for help—after all, I was supposed to be the lifesaver, and I had looked forward to working as a lifeguard. However, as I saw my need, I realized I would have been stupid to pretend to be okay, all set, and in control.

When God calls us to become like little children, I believe one of the qualities he calls us to imitate is their eagerness to ask for help. I often hear the words, "Help me, Nana!" They are spoken with humility, and with the confidence and trust that I am bigger and wiser than my grandchildren—and therefore able to help them.

There are many times and situations in life when all I know to say to God is "Help me!" These words come more easily when I am aware that I am not in control. However, too often I forget that I am never really in control and that every breath I take is dependent upon him.

> "'For in him we live and move and have our being.' As some of your own poets have said, 'We are his offspring.'" (Acts 17:28)

I realize that a "help me" posture toward God is the one with which I need to begin and end every day, not just the days when I feel desperate. As Jehoshaphat said in 2 Chronicles 20:12,

> "O our God, will you not judge them? For we have no power to face this vast army that is attacking us. We do not know what to do, but our eyes are upon you."

The truth is, without God's leadership and presence in my life, every moment is desperate. I don't know what to do without God, and I am so grateful that I can look to him for help. My God is eager to answer my call for help.

As I sat in the lifeguard's chair today, it was a good reminder to me that I am always in desperate need of God's help.

> "I took you from the ends of the earth,
>   from its farthest corners I called you.
> I said, 'You are my servant';
>   I have chosen you and have not rejected you.
> So do not fear, for I am with you;
>   do not be dismayed, for I am your God.
> I will strengthen you **and help you**;
>   I will uphold you with my righteous right hand."
> (Isaiah 41:9–10, emphasis added)

> So they brought him. When the spirit saw Jesus, it immediately threw the boy into a convulsion. He fell to the ground and rolled around, foaming at the mouth.
> Jesus asked the boy's father, "How long has he been like this?"
>   "From childhood," he answered. "It has often thrown him into fire or water to kill him. But if you can do anything, take pity on us and **help us**."
>   "If you can?" said Jesus. "Everything is possible for him who believes."
>   Immediately the boy's father exclaimed, "I do believe; **help me** overcome my unbelief!" (Mark 9:20–24, emphasis added)

> They were all filled with awe and praised God. "A great prophet has appeared among us," they said. "**God has come to help** his people." (Luke 7:16, emphasis added)
>
> So we say with confidence, "**The Lord is my helper;** I will not be afraid." (Hebrews 13:6, emphasis added)

I pray that the phrase "help me" is a regular part of my vocabulary and posture toward God.

dog and pony show 70

Do you ever find yourself in situations where you are in over your head? Sometimes my learning curve is steep. Such was the case when I began an eight-year stint working for a wonderful non-profit, HOPE Worldwide. During this time my eyes were opened to many things. First were the living conditions of the majority of the world's population. I visited slums worldwide and met many amazing and grateful people—despite their destitute conditions. I cried more tears than I had ever cried before.

Second on the learning curve was how much I had to learn about my new job. The philanthropic world of non-profits was new to me. I figured a 501(c)(3) was either a locker combination or a new model of Nissan. I had to learn that an NGO was not text slang for "never getting old," and inurement wasn't something cows left on the ground. Also, grant writing did not mean sending an e-mail to my nephew, Grant.

My naivete amused my colleagues. When I joined in a discussion about a kickoff for a new program and the need to make a certain event a "dog and pony show," my wheels started turning. I thought it was a strange idea—but hey, I loved dogs and horses, so why not have a fundraiser using these fine specimens from the animal kingdom? I soon learned that a dog and pony show was not—er, ahem, gulp— well, it was not a real dog

and pony show. I have to say I was a little disappointed about that. It could have been fun.

The next item on the learning curve agenda came during a trip to Washington, DC. I had actually learned quite a lot by this point in time; however I could still describe this trip as *Ernest Goes to Washington*. You've heard of the movie *Mr. Smith Goes to Washington?* Mr. Smith's trip went well... but you may also remember a goofy movie character from the 1980s, Ernest P. Worrell. If *Ernest* went to Washington... heaven help our country.

Since I was working to help establish programs to help the poor (particularly in Eastern Europe), I was invited to a United Nations advisory council meeting for Eastern Europe held on Capitol Hill. I had become an official representative for this advisory council and would go to learn and to contribute. For some reason (still unknown to me today), on the first day of the meeting I volunteered to be something for which I don't even remember the name. I soon came to learn that it involved summarizing everyone's comments and presenting them to the group in an organized fashion—United Nations style (whatever that was).

During the first break, I found my friend Kitty (Kitty is a person, not a feline), who had many more years of experience in this kind of work than I had. Unfortunately for me, she was involved in a different meeting. I confided that I had just volunteered for something that I had no idea how to do. She gave me a few pointers and a look that said, "Good luck... and are you crazy?!"

So I did the only reasonable thing to do. I went into the bathroom stall and begged God for wisdom and help so I could better help the poor and not reflect badly on my organization (or make a fool out of myself).

> If any of you lacks wisdom, he should ask God, who gives generously to all without finding fault, and it will be given to him. But when he asks, he must believe and not doubt, because he who doubts is like a wave of the sea, blown and tossed by the wind. That man should not think he will

receive anything from the Lord; he is a double-minded man, unstable in all he does. (James 1:5–8)

As soon as I walked out of the stall, some unknown woman came up to me and said, "I don't know how you are handling this presentation, but if I were doing it here is exactly what I would say."

I don't know if she saw the look of total shock on my face. I told her I would consider her words, and then feverishly wrote down everything she said.

Not only did I say all she had said to me, but I also realized that because I was the only one in the room who had actually spent time with the poor in Eastern Europe, I really did have something to offer. I also learned a crucial lesson. God blesses requests for wisdom without laughing at us or "finding fault," just as the scripture says. I rely on this promise often, realizing that when I am trying to serve God and step forward in faith, not knowing where to step next, God always comes through. One of my favorite quotes is entitled "Faith," by Patrick Overton:

> "When you come to the edge of all the light you have
> And take the first step into the darkness of the unknown
> You must believe one of two things will happen:
> There will be something solid for you to stand upon,
> or you will be taught how to fly."

upstairs water   71

"I want downstairs water! I don't want upstairs water!"

These were the words my granddaughter screamed. I laughed out loud as my daughter described her three-year-old's tantrum and the discipline that followed. I reminisced about my daughter at that age—fiercely holding to her resolve that she was thirsty, but absolutely refusing water I offered her from the bathroom sink. Only kitchen water would do! She would not back down until she was absolutely and completely convinced that she could not win the battle (at times after hours of being disciplined—yes, seriously—hours). Wow, those battles were intense and required lots of prayer and an accompanying forehead of flint! I often gained courage from God's words to Ezekiel:

> "But the house of Israel is not willing to listen to you because they are not willing to listen to me, for the whole house of Israel is hardened and obstinate. But I will make you as unyielding and hardened as they are. I will make your forehead like the hardest stone, harder than flint. Do not be afraid of them or terrified by them, though they are a rebellious house." (Ezekiel 3:7–9)

These showdowns were not much fun at the time, but as I look back at my children and now watch my grandchildren, I'm amused at our children's propensity to think something that they can't have is so much better than what is offered and available to them. They are with every breath saying, "I want it my way, thank you."

As I now observe the scene in front of me I see the "same song, different verse." Our puppy, Denver, has a wonderful and comfortable pillow-lined crate. Blackie (our little dog) was acting envious of Denver's crate, and would sometimes climb in and take over the space. So I, being a compassionate doggie parent, recently purchased a small doggie bed for Blackie. He was thrilled and immediately tucked himself in. When he  got up for a moment, he lost his spot on the bed. Denver wanted Blackie's new bed, and so plopped right down and fell asleep. Blackie stared at him and snarled.

As I mulled over my granddaughter's stubborn desire for something other than what she was offered, and my pup's desire for what the older dog had, I was reminded of how easy it is to become discontent with what is offered to us. It's easy to become discontent: with the weather, our work, our health, and all kinds of things. Surely "downstairs water" would be much better than "upstairs water," and the other dog's bed would be much more comfortable. When I become discontent, I'm afraid it looks too much like these toddler and doggie scenarios. That is when I must remind myself of scriptures such as Psalm 23:1–2:

> The LORD is my shepherd, I shall not be in want.
>   He makes me lie down in green pastures,
> he leads me beside quiet waters.
>
> The fear of the LORD leads to life:
>   Then one rests content, untouched by trouble.
> (Proverbs 19:23)
>
> I am not saying this because I am in need, for I have learned to be content whatever the circumstances. I know what it is to be in need, and I know what it is to have

plenty. I have learned the secret of being content in any and every situation, whether well fed or hungry, whether living in plenty or in want. (Philippians 4:11–12)

But godliness with contentment is great gain.
(1 Timothy 6:6)

Keep your lives free from the love of money and be content with what you have, because God has said,

"Never will I leave you;
 never will I forsake you." (Hebrews 13:5)

May I always be grateful for "upstairs water!"

be still and... juggle? 72

My favorite breakfast place opened this weekend. It's a place where I enjoy breakfast at a table that overlooks the vast expanse of the North Atlantic. I took the morning off in order to visit this special spot. I had extra time to meditate on "life and godliness" as I drank my coffee. Wyndham is usually with me on these visits, but this time I went by myself (well, God was with me). As the only patron in the restaurant (this is the very early season), I appreciated the opportunity to practice the scripture in Psalm 46:10–11:

> "Be still, and know that I am God;
>   I will be exalted among the nations,
>   I will be exalted in the earth."
> The LORD Almighty is with us;
>   the God of Jacob is our fortress.

So often, life moves at such a fast pace that it is hard to simply be still and reflect on who God is. I thought of ways he shows himself through Jesus as our Mighty God, Everlasting Father, Wonderful Counselor, and Prince of Peace. As I thought through these descriptions of my God, I felt extremely grateful for all of these ways that he interacts with me.

As I sipped my coffee and looked out over the expanse of blue, my eyes caught sight of something outside of the window that I must say I have never seen before. A man was jogging— not so strange. But this man was also juggling three or four tennis balls! He didn't miss a stride or a tennis ball. I was amazed. I hate jogging, and it takes every ounce of concentration and determination I can muster to keep moving. Yet this guy was not only moving at a rapid pace, but his juggling seemed effortless. (He was too fast for me to catch with my camera.)

I laughed (to myself since no one else was there), thinking about the contrast of what I was doing versus what he was doing. I also thought about how his actions portrayed the way that life so often feels. I can often feel like I am juggling while running. I don't think I am unusual in my efforts to keep numerous "balls" in the air without dropping them, while at the same time running from one thing to the next.

I need the strength of the Mighty God, the wisdom of the Wonderful Counselor, the steadiness of the Everlasting Father, and the trust in the Prince of Peace to be able to combine the stillness of soul that I felt as I looked out of the window with the crazy activity of running and juggling that I viewed from that same window.

After finishing my breakfast, I took a long walk so that I could pray, smell the salt air, feel the breeze, and watch the ocean waves push against the protruding rocks. As I prayed about the many things on my heart, I thought of the times I get too busy running and juggling. Two scriptures help to ground me and help me to discern whether my running and juggling have gotten out of balance. I meditated on these scriptures as I walked and prayed.

The first is one I must read often, as I tend to be more like Martha, and yet need to be more like Mary, who chose what is best:

> As Jesus and his disciples were on their way, he came to a village where a woman named Martha opened her home to him. She had a sister called Mary, who sat at the

> Lord's feet listening to what he said. But Martha was distracted by all the preparations that had to be made. She came to him and asked, "Lord, don't you care that my sister has left me to do the work by myself? Tell her to help me!"
>
> "Martha, Martha," the Lord answered, "you are worried and upset about many things, but only one thing is needed. Mary has chosen what is better, and it will not be taken away from her." (Luke 10:38–42)

This following scripture helps me discern whether or not my busyness is merely activity, or if it is in keeping with seeking first God's choices and desires.

> "But seek first his kingdom and his righteousness, and all these things will be given to you as well. Therefore do not worry about tomorrow, for tomorrow will worry about itself. Each day has enough trouble of its own."
> (Matthew 6:33–34)

I pray that as I juggle and jog in my daily activities I will see God for who he really is—and that my purpose, priorities, and desires are united with his. Then, even amidst the busyness, I can be still and know that he is God.

closer than a tick on a hound dog   73

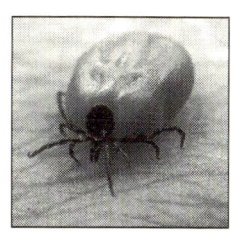

I've never been fond of ticks. I once accidentally picked up a well-fed tick from my kitchen floor, thinking I had dropped a blueberry. That discovery was thoroughly disgusting; it was a while before I was able to eat a blueberry again. Most ticks, however, are smaller than blueberries and often go unnoticed.

I live in the midst of tick country. Lyme, Connecticut, is not far from my home, and the Northeast corridor where I live is known for its disease-carrying ticks. Our dogs receive a Lyme vaccine each year and we use a tick preventative on their fur coats for extra protection. I'm careful to watch for ticks on their skin—but I guess I should have put some of their prevention medicine on my skin. Somewhere, sometime in the recent past, I evidently had a tick attach itself to me. I never knew it was there, yet it snuck in and wreaked havoc in my body.

As I shared in earlier chapters, I recently had a heart catheter ablation. It was a needed and successful procedure, but after it was over I began to feel even worse. I read Internet postings from other people who have undergone this procedure to see if they felt the same way I did, and was befuddled by their joyful comments about how their hearts were now quiet. I was happy for them, but I knew something was wrong with me.

Shortly after my ablation, I was longing for that quiet heart. My heart felt anything but quiet. I couldn't sleep most nights, and felt like I was wired to an IV full of adrenaline mixed with caffeine. I felt my heart beating through my eyelids, fingertips, ears, and throat. My body would involuntarily start to shake. My pulse rose, and so did my blood pressure. I should have taken orders for overnight house cleaning, gardening, and all kinds of physical labor, as I felt like I was on overdrive. I was miserable! I found some relief from a prescribed medication, but unfortunately, it was only treating the symptoms. I begged God for relief, most nights listening to music to try to gain some distraction. I watched more late night/early morning Food Network shows like *Chopped* and *Cupcake Wars* than I care to remember.

Today I saw my primary care physician and my cardiologist. (Yes, the one with the 1950s office.) I'm grateful for an astute physician who followed her hunch. She had a premonition of what could be at the root of things and ordered a test: a Western Blot Lyme disease test. It was positive, and I was diagnosed with an acute case of Lyme disease. A tick—or rather, the infection the tick had left behind, had messed with my heart. The doctors conjectured that the prodding from the heart procedure had awakened the infection and caused these difficult episodes.

After my heart rate normalizes, I can begin the Lyme disease treatment, and expect full and complete recovery! Two scriptural principles stand out to me as I think of these new developments.

> "They dress the wound of my people
>   as though it were not serious.
> 'Peace, peace,' they say,
>   when there is no peace.
> Are they ashamed of their loathsome conduct?
>   No, they have no shame at all;
>   they do not even know how to blush.
> So they will fall among the fallen;
>   they will be brought down when I punish them,"
>   says the LORD.

This is what the LORD says:

> "Stand at the crossroads and look;
>   ask for the ancient paths,

> ask where the good way is, and walk in it,
> and you will find rest for your souls." (Jeremiah 6:14–16)

This scripture teaches me that it does no good to put spiritual Band-Aids over spiritual, emotional, or physical issues that must be addressed at the root. It is harmful tell people they are okay with God, if in fact God's own words may say differently. We must "test" our lives with God's word to know the good way, to choose it and walk in it. This choice can give us rest for our souls.

Proverbs 20:5 teaches me that I need others in my life to help me "diagnose" the things in my heart.

> The purposes of a man's heart are deep waters,
> but a man of understanding draws them out.

I am grateful for the woman of medical understanding who looked deeper than the surface. I'm also grateful for the people who help me diagnose my spiritual heart.

it's battle time! 74

It had begun as a silent battle. I didn't know I was being invaded by the dark side: the Borrelia burgdorferi spirochete. These are the corkscrew-shaped bacteria that cause Lyme disease. I've learned a lot about Lyme disease these past few weeks. For instance, I didn't know the disease could target certain areas of the body, like the heart. With their spiral twirls, the bacteria often strangle nerves and wreak havoc on people's health. In a twisted sort of way, I'm very grateful for the miserable heart procedure I had about six weeks ago. After my catheter ablation, these bacteria guys got angry. If I hadn't undergone that procedure, these mean little spirochetes may have kept on gathering allies, silently setting the stage for a full-out war on my health. I had no idea who these guys were and that they were hiding out in my heart. But now I know—and the battle is on!

My physicians informed me that the Lyme disease treatment might cause my heart and body to feel a little "funky" for a while during the initial time when the bacteria were dying off. (In my experience, "funky" is medical jargon for "utterly miserable.") I stored that information in my mind, and this week I began a long course of antibiotics, which will increase in dosage over time. (Whew—the natural frozen yogurt store opened in my town in the knick of time—I will obviously need those live yogurt cultures with probiotics to balance out the antibiotics, right?)

As the doctors forewarned, since beginning the course of antibiotics, I have been awakened in the middle of the night by heart flutters, and by the strange sense of activity going on inside of my body. It feels sort of like something is attacking something else. (I know, my medical vocabulary is astounding!) This feeling actually encourages me, as it tells me that the bad guys are going down.

I feel very thankful. If I had continued without knowledge of the presence of these bad guys, they would have caused increasing damage. Now I know they are present—and with proper weapons we can take them down!

I think of the spiritual war that goes on in our hearts day after day, often unseen. If I remain unaware of the spiritual battle, I will be defenseless as the forces of evil hold me captive. However, from God's word I learn his plan for my life and how to experience the power to change and live a life that is complete, fulfilled, and pleasing to him. I can be armed... and take down the "dark side." At times I can feel the strains of battle, but I know who ultimately wins!

> Finally, be strong in the Lord and in his mighty power. Put on the full armor of God so that you can take your stand against the devil's schemes. For our struggle is not against flesh and blood, but against the rulers, against the authorities, against the powers of this dark world and against the spiritual forces of evil in the heavenly realms. Therefore put on the full armor of God, so that when the day of evil comes, you may be able to stand your ground, and after you have done everything, to stand. Stand firm then, with the belt of truth buckled around your waist, with the breastplate of righteousness in place, and with your feet fitted with the readiness that comes from the gospel of peace. In addition to all this, take up the shield of faith, with which you can extinguish all the flaming arrows of the evil one. Take the helmet of salvation and the sword of

the Spirit, which is the word of God. And pray in the Spirit on all occasions with all kinds of prayers and requests. With this in mind, be alert and always keep on praying for all the saints. (Ephesians 6:10–18)

You, dear children, are from God and have overcome them, because the one who is in you is greater than the one who is in the world. (1 John 4:4)

noticing life 75

"This is why I speak to them in parables:

'Though seeing, they do not see;
though hearing, they do not hear or understand.'"
(Matthew 13:13)

I thought I noticed most things that go on around me—that is, until today.

Since my daughter had a Bible study with her neighbor this morning, I offered to watch her son for several hours. I had errands to run, so I took Micah with me to the post office, gas station, and grocery store. I marveled at all that Micah noticed while we traveled from place to place. He didn't miss a thing! Usually, I get in the car and basically drive on autopilot. I stare into space while I pump gas, and then move quickly through the market while trying to remember the things I need to purchase. Where I can be oblivious to the details of life around me, my grandson missed nothing. I came away from this time resolved to be more alert to people and situations around me, and to see them through Jesus' eyes. I certainly don't want to see, but not really see; or hear, but not really hear.

When I pulled into the parking lot, I quickly transcribed all that I remembered of Micah's commentary from our ten-minute, three-mile drive. I didn't want to forget this stream of conversation. Micah's reporting began as we pulled out of his driveway. It went something like this:

There's my park Nana. I like to play at the park. I like to slide. There are lots of cars on the road. Vroom, vroom.

I'm on my side in the back seat. You are on your side, Nana. There's a dozer there. (Micah calls bulldozers "dozers.") *What's that noise? There's a mailman. Are we going to the mailman's house? Are you going down a hill now? Who's that in Mommy's car?* (He spotted a car like his mommy drives a few cars ahead of us.) *Prob'ly a lady in there. Are we going by the fire trucks?* (We were nearing the road that leads to the fire station.) *What are those guys doing?* (I didn't see the guys he was talking about, so I asked him what guys he was talking about. He responded by answering his own question.) *Those guys workin' in the dump truck.*

As we approached the post office: *I'm excited to get out. Does the mailman live here?*

Inside the post office, Micah had a lot to say to me and to the other post office patrons: *What are you doing? What are you doing? What are you doing now? What are you doing?*

As we got back in the car and turned the corner where there is a train station: *There's the train station. I won't be scared when the train comes. I'll wait to ride with my dad. I'm going to wait for the train and go to the city of Boston.*

There's an ambulance. There's a digger. I want to go see the digger. Let's go see the digger.

Happy Mother's Day, Nana. (Big smile.)

Inside the grocery store, we went to the seafood counter to buy fish. Meanwhile, Micah talked to all the women at the counter, and admired the fish on display. *Nana, are you getting Nemo?*

If I'd done my errands by myself, I would have missed ninety percent (or more!) of the things, people, and sounds that Micah saw and heard. Listening to Micah's running commentary and questions made me much more aware of people I could meet and lessons I could learn. I suddenly began viewing my surroundings through the fresh, eager eyes of a two-year-old who was eager to take in everything around him.

I went to my Bible tonight to seek to learn from the ways Jesus noticed people and situations, and the ways he responded to them. He saw the people behind the situations. Jesus noticed people's plights, distress, faith, and lack of faith. He responded with what they needed. Take a look at a few examples:

> When Jesus came into Peter's house, he saw Peter's mother-in-law lying in bed with a fever. (Matthew 8:14)

> Some men brought to him a paralytic, lying on a mat. When Jesus saw their faith, he said to the paralytic, "Take heart, son; your sins are forgiven." (Matthew 9:2)

> When he saw the crowds, he had compassion on them, because they were harassed and helpless, like sheep without a shepherd. (Matthew 9:36)

> When they came to the home of the synagogue ruler, Jesus saw a commotion, with people crying and wailing loudly. He went in and said to them, "Why all this commotion and wailing? The child is not dead but asleep." But they laughed at him.
> After he put them all out, he took the child's father and mother and the disciples who were with him, and went in where the child was. He took her by the hand and said to her, *"Talitha koum!"* (which means, "Little girl, I say to you, get up!"). (Mark 5:38–41)

> When Jesus saw this, he was indignant. He said to them, "Let the little children come to me, and do not hinder them, for the kingdom of God belongs to such as these." (Mark 10:14)

> Jesus looked at him and loved him. "One thing you lack," he said. "Go, sell everything you have and give to the poor, and you will have treasure in heaven. Then come, follow me." (Mark 10:21)

When Jesus saw their faith, he said, "Friend, your sins are forgiven." (Luke 5:20)

Jesus looked at him and said, "How hard it is for the rich to enter the kingdom of God!" (Luke 18:24)

He saw through their duplicity and said to them, "Show me a denarius. Whose portrait and inscription are on it?" (Luke 20:23–24)

As he looked up, Jesus saw the rich putting their gifts into the temple treasury. He also saw a poor widow put in two very small copper coins. "I tell you the truth," he said, "this poor widow has put in more than all the others. All these people gave their gifts out of their wealth; but she out of her poverty put in all she had to live on." (Luke 21:1–4)

When Jesus saw him lying there and learned that he had been in this condition for a long time, he asked him, "Do you want to get well?" (John 5:6)

When Jesus saw her weeping, and the Jews who had come along with her also weeping, he was deeply moved in spirit and troubled. (John 11:33)

Thanks, Micah, for calling me higher today by helping me notice things through your fresh and eager eyes. May I seek to respond to what I see in the loving and courageous ways that Jesus did. May I look, and really see; may I listen, and really hear.

filling the birdfeeder   76

For my birthday last year my family gave me some money. I had planned to put it toward an iPad or similar electronic tablet. After researching numerous options, I scurried to the mall to purchase my gift from the family. I looked and looked for the best one to purchase, and debated with myself over the many options available.

Three hours later, I returned home with five birdfeeders. You see, I realized that I might not actually like the electronic tablet. I  use my laptop consistently, and I am comfortable with it. I can carry it on trips, and I could even use it on the front porch while admiring the flowers and birds—if only I had birdfeeders with which to attract some birds! (Logical train of thought, right?) And so I veered from the Apple store to the hardware store.

I was thrilled with my purchases: a new super-duper birdfeeder for the back deck; a yellow feeder designed for yellow finches; a simple birdhouse for viewing birds outside the kitchen window, and a couple of hummingbird feeders. I hung them all and waited for the birds to arrive. They came, and I'm sure I've enjoyed them more than a tablet (which I got for Christmas after all).

This morning I was reminded of my unexpected purchase as I watched some beautiful yellow finches arrive at the new feeder on my front porch. The one I'd originally bought was defective and had to be replaced. The openings on the defective feeder were not set up correctly, and birdseed spilled out of the openings as fast as I could pour the food in. I tried several times, thinking that perhaps I was pouring it wrong—but alas, it just kept falling out onto the porch and the yard. The spilled birdseed left a pile of mess.

Our lives can at times seem like this broken birdfeeder. Due to losses, rejection, unresolved issues from our past, or simply a failure to seek God first, we can have spiritual "holes" in our souls that keep us from being "filled up." We may try to fill these voids with accomplishments, relationships, and material things. But these things don't fulfill us. We try again and again to fill ourselves up, only to be left with a mess.

> When a Samaritan woman came to draw water, Jesus said to her, "Will you give me a drink?" (His disciples had gone into the town to buy food.)
> The Samaritan woman said to him, "You are a Jew and I am a Samaritan woman. How can you ask me for a drink?" (For Jews do not associate with Samaritans.)
> Jesus answered her, "If you knew the gift of God and who it is that asks you for a drink, you would have asked him and he would have given you living water."
> "Sir," the woman said, "you have nothing to draw with and the well is deep. Where can you get this living water? Are you greater than our father Jacob, who gave us the well and drank from it himself, as did also his sons and his flocks and herds?"
> Jesus answered, "Everyone who drinks this water will be thirsty again, but whoever drinks the water I give him will never thirst. Indeed, the water I give him will become in him a spring of water welling up to eternal life."
> (John 4:7–14)

This is an amazing claim and promise from Jesus. I have found his words to be true in my life again and again. A true relationship with Jesus is the only thing that makes me complete in the depths of my soul. If I try to fill my life with anything other than Jesus, it just spills out and leaves a mess. I love this life-giving water that completes me and never runs dry.

a bird on the head   77

I was visiting my friend when her bird flew from its cage and perched atop my head. It was a little weird to feel tiny bird feet in my hair, but I wasn't overly concerned. After all, what could a little bird do?

My friend soon came to my rescue and gathered her bird in her hand (which I've heard is worth two in the bush). Before she took the bird, I told her I was okay with the situation, as long as the bird didn't poop in my hair. She stopped for a moment and said in a quiet voice, "Well, it looks like it's too late for that."

So that's what a little bird can do.

"Uh-oh," I thought. I had let the bird stay a little too long in my hair. I should have reacted sooner.

So it is with the way of temptation. We can let it sit a little too long and end up with a situation much worse than poop in our hair.

When we are tempted, the best plan is the one we hear from our brother Paul in 1 Timothy 6:11 and again in 2 Timothy 2:22. Both times, Paul tells us to run away from temptation.

James tells us that when we let temptation conceive, burrow in our hearts and grow, it soon becomes sin.

> When tempted, no one should say, "God is tempting me." For God cannot be tempted by evil, nor does he tempt anyone; but each one is tempted when, by his own evil desire, he is dragged away and enticed. Then, after desire has conceived, it gives birth to sin; and sin, when it is full-grown, gives birth to death. (James 1:13–15)

When our hearts are slow to forgive, this also gives time for sin to nest (or worse). Hebrews 12:15 states,

> See to it that no one misses the grace of God and that no bitter root grows up to cause trouble and defile many.

When we are slow to forgive, we end up with very unfortunate consequences, much worse than any bird can produce. We can not only miss God's grace, but end up hurting other people with our bitterness.

While I didn't love the poop that settled on my head, this little bird reminded me of the lesson to always be urgent in shooing temptation away. A lackadaisical attitude can end up defiling us and harming others as well. Now that's a bona fide mess that will take more than a little shampoo to clean up!

go ahead... I'm covered! 78

I felt something behind my knee, and kept swiping at it. I felt it again—and upon further exploration, found a tick hanging out on my leg. You might be thinking: What in the world is going on with me and the ticks? I don't have fur and I don't live in the woods! However, I often walk outdoors; I also have two dogs and I live in the heart of tick country. So I guess I will continue to be a prime candidate for tick bites.

As I grabbed the tick and prepared to send him swirling down the porcelain throne, I boldly told him, "Go ahead and bite me—I'm covered!"

The tick said nothing in return. He had no answer.

You see, I am in my third month of treatment for Lyme disease. I take three antibiotics a day. While I hope the end of the treatment is in sight, right now I'm still being treated, so I feel confident in my immunity to this tick's attack. I don't know if my feeling is medically sound, but I know I'm "antibiotically covered." Lyme bacteria may try to infiltrate me, but they won't stick!

This little visit with the tick reminded me of the scripture in 1 John 1:6–7:

> If we claim to have fellowship with him yet walk in the darkness, we lie and do not live by the truth. But if we walk in the light, as he is in the light, we have fellowship with one another, and the blood of Jesus, his Son, purifies us from all sin.

I've got God's Spirit in me. I'm purposely walking in the light, so even when I mess up while I'm trying to follow Jesus, I'm continually cleansed from sin. This fact gives me great comfort.

This scripture was further reinforced in my mind as I recently went to run some errands in inclement weather. It was raining. As I drove down the interstate, the rain seemed to come down harder and harder. I was grateful for good windshield wipers. I turned them on faster, and they kept wiping away the rain so I could see clearly despite the weather.

The scripture in 1 John also reminds me of the windshield wipers. Just as windshield wipers keep wiping away the rain so I can see clearly, so the blood of Jesus that covered me when I was baptized (and keeps covering me as I walk in the light) continually cleanses me.

So go on tick—bite me. I'm covered. And go ahead rain—keep on falling. My windshield wipers are going strong.

As this book goes to press I am happy to report that the six months of antibiotics have given me a clean bill of health. No more Lyme!

team band-aid 79

Our annual Summer Vacation Olympics was finally here. The grounds were set up for the games. My son, Sam (a.k.a. the Gamemaster), had set up the different stations and gathered the needed supplies. The cameras were ready, and we were set for a fun time of craziness. We divided up into two teams and were ready to commence the games... almost.

As we gathered into our teams, my granddaughter Emma hung back. Her teammates noticed that she was feeling a little insecure about the bandage on her face. The previous night had ended with a fun time of s'mores around a fire pit, but the fun had turned to pain when Emma's stick broke just as she was pulling a perfectly toasted marshmallow out of the fire. As it broke, the smoldering marshmallow flew off the stick onto Emma's cheek. She was left with a painful burn that quickly blistered her beautiful skin. (Thankfully, the burn healed well within the week.) Her cheek had to be coated with an antibiotic and then bandaged. She was not thrilled about the idea of being photographed during the Crazy Olympics.

Quickly, almost without thinking, the rest of her team hurried into the house and soon came back out with their faces bandaged just like Emma's. They called themselves Team Band-Aid. We all laughed, and the games began in a spirit of unity.

I was moved by this act of unity for the sake of a team member, and was reminded of two scriptures that teach this concept:

> Though I am free and belong to no man, I make myself a slave to everyone, to win as many as possible. To the Jews I became like a Jew, to win the Jews. To those under the law I became like one under the law (though I myself am not under the law), so as to win those under the law. To those not having the law I became like one not having the law (though I am not free from God's law but am under Christ's law), so as to win those not having the law. To the weak I became weak, to win the weak. I have become all things to all men so that by all possible means I might save some. I do all this for the sake of the gospel, that I may share in its blessings. (1 Corinthians 9:19–23)

> The eye cannot say to the hand, "I don't need you!" And the head cannot say to the feet, "I don't need you!" On the contrary, those parts of the body that seem to be weaker are indispensable, and the parts that we think are less honorable we treat with special honor. And the parts that are unpresentable are treated with special modesty, while our presentable parts need no special treatment. But God has combined the members of the body and has given greater honor to the parts that lacked it, so that there should be no division in the body, but that its parts should have equal concern for each other. If one part suffers, every part suffers with it; if one part is honored, every part rejoices with it. (1 Corinthians 12:21–26)

The first scripture challenges my heart to listen, connect, notice, and seek to understand the thoughts and challenges of others. I can sometimes see someone's different ways of thinking about or viewing things and think, "What's wrong with them?" Instead, I want to understand and draw them out and toward Jesus.

The second scripture reminds me to not only be considerate toward other disciples (even in their weaknesses), but to also appreciate others, learn from them, and realize my need for all members of the body. In this way, I can truly rejoice with those who rejoice and hurt with those who hurt.

I pray that I can notice the hurts, insecurities, and joys of people around me, and meet them wherever they are—encouraging them and drawing them out as needed. I know that's how I want to be treated. I'm so grateful that Jesus treats me this way. I am inspired by Team Band-Aid. May I be quick to run to the house to grab my Band-Aid in order to become all things to all people.

dive in 80

It was my turn. All the other family members had taken the plunge in our annual Summer Vacation Crazy Olympics. I was happy to be the photographer, reporter, cheerleader, whatever—just not the participant. I don't mind diving into water (as long as it's not too cold), but I wasn't too sure about diving into the ground. But it seemed this was a necessary part of the event.

This "Human Bowling" event entailed taking a plunging slide down the Slip 'N Slide in order to knock over boxes that had been set up as bowling pins. I was a bit fearful of getting hurt on the plunge, but mostly, I was hesitant because of the frigid water on the slide. You see, I like my water comfortably warm, and even then I take my time to meander in so I can "get used to it."

The more I thought about the process, the more difficult it seemed. I hesitated. I heard the family's chants of "Nana, Nana, Nana," which were partly encouraging and partly annoying. I did not want to let the team down, but couldn't I fade into the background just this once? So as a compromise, I ran down beside the slide with my foot in the water, hoping that would count. Alas, it did not.

I sought to learn from this struggle. I've been reading the Old Testament of late, and these lessons touched my heart:

> So Ahab sent word throughout all Israel and assembled the prophets on Mount Carmel. Elijah went before the people and said, "How long will you waver between two opinions? If the LORD is God, follow him; but if Baal is God, follow him."
> But the people said nothing. (1 Kings 18:20–21)

Elijah's question to the crowd, "How long will you waver between two opinions?" was far-reaching. Those who wavered witnessed defeat. Those who followed the Lord wholeheartedly saw God move powerfully.

> "But because my servant Caleb has a different spirit and follows me wholeheartedly, I will bring him into the land he went to, and his descendants will inherit it."
> (Numbers 14:24)

And this "different spirit" followed Caleb later in his life as we see him in Joshua 14:10–12:

> "Now then, just as the LORD promised, he has kept me alive for forty-five years since the time he said this to Moses, while Israel moved about in the desert. So here I am today, eighty-five years old! I am still as strong today as the day Moses sent me out; I'm just as vigorous to go out to battle now as I was then. Now give me this hill country that the LORD promised me that day. You yourself heard then that the Anakites were there and their cities were large and fortified, but, the LORD helping me, I will drive them out just as he said."

So, with inspiration from Elijah and Caleb (and my cheering family), I dove in. I made a decision to no longer hesitate, waver between two opinions, or be a "has-been" participant holding back in my comfort zone. The plunge felt like a moment of reckless abandon, but I am grateful I took it. It wasn't pretty, but it was fulfilling.

More importantly, may I never hesitate, waver between two opinions, or lose my eagerness and passion to keep going and growing in my spiritual walk.

If you are wavering or hesitant to go forward with a decision, take a lesson from Human Bowling. Just dive on in. You will be glad you did.

izzy dizzy 81

Our favorite event was at hand. This event, dubbed the Izzy Dizzy Race, humiliates me every year—and makes us laugh until we cry. The directions for this relay race go like this: Place your forehead on a bat, hold the bat on the ground, spin around the bat five times, run across the field to a plate filled with gummy worms covered with whipped cream, dig your face into the cream until you find a gummy worm, carry your gummy worm in your teeth as you run back to pass it on to the next team member, and  then your team member must eat the gummy worm before spinning around the bat himself...

The problem is, I can't complete five spins without falling to the ground like a drunken fool. If I try to get up, I fall again. So I have to crawl to get to the goal. The younger kids, being closer to the ground, are the best at this race. The adults fall over, run into the trees or bushes, or just stagger off course until they gain their stability.

The Izzy Dizzy race reminds me of the scripture in 1 Corinthians:

> Do you not know that in a race all the runners run, but only one gets the prize? Run in such a way as to get the prize. Everyone who competes in the games goes into strict

> training. They do it to get a crown that will not last; but we do it to get a crown that will last forever. Therefore I do not run like a man running aimlessly; I do not fight like a man beating the air. No, I beat my body and make it my slave so that after I have preached to others, I myself will not be disqualified for the prize. (1 Corinthians 9:24–27)

I am challenged by the charge to run in such a way as to get the prize. I don't want to run my spiritual race like I run the Izzy Dizzy race! However, whenever I get distracted from my goals—of being with Jesus forever in heaven, becoming more like him, and bringing others to him—I can do just that. If I look down and fix my eyes on my circumstances or the physical things around me, and if I "attach my head" to those things, I don't get very far spiritually. In fact, I spin in circles and fall down. I must keep my eyes on the goal and keep trying to get up and get to the goal, even if I have to crawl or continually correct my course.

But I can't reach my goal alone. I appreciate and need the people who cheer me on.

> Therefore, since we are surrounded by such a great cloud of witnesses, let us throw off everything that hinders and the sin that so easily entangles, and let us run with perseverance the race marked out for us. Let us fix our eyes on Jesus, the author and perfecter of our faith, who for the joy set before him endured the cross, scorning its shame, and sat down at the right hand of the throne of God. Consider him who endured such opposition from sinful men, so that you will not grow weary and lose heart.
> (Hebrews 12:1–3)

As I fix my eyes on Jesus, I take comfort in the knowledge that he always "makes my path straight," no matter how much Satan tries to spin me around.

painting Papa's toenails 82

After an early morning of fishing and lots of activity throughout the day, Wyndham (the grandkids call him "Papa") had fallen asleep right in the middle of the chaos of the living room "playground." Some of the girls had given themselves manicures earlier in the day, so the "evil painting tools" were within easy access.

Papa's sleepy and exposed toes just seemed to be begging for attention from the grandchildren. The kids decided on the bright red nail polish, and with many muffled giggles they staged a full frontal attack on Papa's toenails. He never even budged. The kids could hardly contain themselves when their little project was completed. After a while, Papa opened one eye, then the other, only to see several little eyes gazing at him, filled with mischief—though he still did not know what they had done. Fortunately for the kids, their Papa is a really good sport, and he took it all in stride. He was particularly grateful that we had nail polish remover on hand, though we hesitated to tell him for a while.

While this is all in fun, it's amazing to think what can happen to our lives when we don't pay attention to what is truly important. The Bible gives us many reminders and warnings about the things that compete for our attention and seek to distract us from what is most important. These passages speak about this:

> "If only you had paid attention to my commands,
> your peace would have been like a river,
> your righteousness like the waves of the sea."
> (Isaiah 48:18)

> "'But they did not listen or pay attention; instead, they followed the stubborn inclinations of their evil hearts. They went backward and not forward.'" (Jeremiah 7:24)

> We must pay more careful attention, therefore, to what we have heard, so that we do not drift away.
> (Hebrews 2:1)

> And we have the word of the prophets made more certain, and you will do well to pay attention to it, as to a light shining in a dark place, until the day dawns and the morning star rises in your hearts. (2 Peter 1:19)

When we are distracted and spiritually asleep, Satan is sure to be crouching at our door. He wants us to lose our souls, so he is delighted any time he finds us with our eyes off of Jesus. He doesn't want to paint our toenails, but he does want to wreak havoc in our lives.

> "If you do what is right, will you not be accepted? But if you do not do what is right, sin is crouching at your door; it desires to have you, but you must master it."
> (Genesis 4:7)

> Be self-controlled and alert. Your enemy the devil prowls around like a roaring lion looking for someone to devour.
> (1 Peter 5:8)

Satan often works to ensure that we stay distracted and aren't awakened to the seriousness of his evil desires. So I have decided to remind myself, whenever I see painted toenails (which is often, since I keep mine painted most of the time), to keep my eyes focused on Jesus and my heart alert to his Word. This awareness can keep me from being lulled to sleep by Satan's schemes.

balderdash 83

I enjoy words, so I'm a big fan of word games. One of my favorite games is called Balderdash. In this game, one person holds the correct definition to a word that most people have never even heard of. The object of the game is to contrive a definition that sounds right, and stump the rest of the players. You receive points for the number of people who believe your definition is correct. We played Balderdash on our family vacation, and laughed a lot at the inventive definitions we all came up with.

Who knew that "dorking" is not the practice of wearing high-water pants and argyle socks, but is actually a five-toed English chicken? Sometimes the truth sounds more fabricated than the lie.

Likewise, Satan feeds us lies that look and sound right. He masquerades as an angel of light (2 Corinthians 11:14).

While Balderdash is played purely for fun, I am reminded of the distress that deceit yields in real life. Satan himself is the master of deceit:

> Jesus said to them, "If God were your Father, you would love me, for I came from God and now am here. I have not come on my own; but he sent me. Why is my language not clear to you? Because you are unable to hear what I say. You belong to your father, the devil, and you

> want to carry out your father's desire. He was a murderer from the beginning, not holding to the truth, for there is no truth in him. When he lies, he speaks his native language, for he is a liar and the father of lies." (John 8:42–44)

It's interesting to think about some of the definitions Satan might give. He would make sinful things sound right and good and wonderful, but his definitions are big fat lies. And these definitions matter—they aren't funny. I can think of so many definitions that he twists. For example:

Happiness, as defined by Satan: A state of being that you can achieve by doing what you feel like doing, whatever way you feel like doing it. After all, you are the most important person in the world and you know what you need.

Identity, as defined by Satan: Our worth as a person—which is based on our wealth, beauty, intelligence, or athletic ability. The pursuit of these qualities deserves our utmost attention, as they define who we really are.

Tomorrow, as defined by Satan: A day in the future that will always be available for us. For this reason we can put off whatever we wish until this day.

Truth, as defined by Satan: The philosophy you embrace—relative to what you think is right and what you choose to believe.

In the game of Balderdash, the only way to determine who is "lying" with their fake definition is by reading the true definition of the word. Likewise, the only way to spot Satan's lies is by learning and knowing the Scriptures. Satan's definitions can sound good and appealing, but the truth is clearly laid out in the Bible. Gaining knowledge of the Scriptures equips us to refute Satan's lies, and this gives us true freedom instead of the warped definitions of freedom that Satan gives.

> To the Jews who had believed him, Jesus said, "If you hold to my teaching, you are really my disciples. Then you will know the truth, and the truth will set you free." (John 8:31–32)

from the lips of children   84

Having finished our picnic this afternoon, my daughters and I were enjoying time together as we admired the beauty of the northern Atlantic. The water sparkled like diamonds and the sun's rays made the cool breeze feel like a kiss on the cheek. We had perfect seats, directly behind two of my grandchildren, who are two and three years old. We were out of their sight, so they were uninhibited by our presence. At one point, we heard singing. Our hearts were warmed as they loudly sang "Jesus Loves Me" and "You Are My Sunshine." Then they continued talking, having a great time. They talked about why they love Jesus. And then part of their conversation went like this:

> Lexi: "You know, Jesus is sad when you are sad. What makes you sad, Micah?"
> Micah: "I'm sad when I have to take nappies."
> Lexi: "So why are you sad when you have to take nappies?"
> (Alas, we couldn't hear Micah's response.)
> Lexi: "Okay, so now we can pray about it."

And then they both folded their hands and prayed! I couldn't hear it all, but the prayer included many things they were thankful for—including the beauty of the place, the warmth, cats and dogs, "persons and kids," and much more.

This moment was beyond precious. I felt like life could not get much better than that moment as I admired the spectacular setting of God's creation and listened to my grandchildren express their love for him and to him. Sometimes, all that seems fitting is praise.

> O LORD, our LORD,
>   how majestic is your name in all the earth!
> You have set your glory
>   above the heavens.
> From the lips of children and infants
>   you have ordained praise
> because of your enemies,
>   to silence the foe and the avenger.
>
> When I consider your heavens,
>   the work of your fingers,
> the moon and the stars,
>   which you have set in place,
> what is man that you are mindful of him,
>   the son of man that you care for him?
> You made him a little lower than the heavenly beings
>   and crowned him with glory and honor.
> You made him ruler over the works of your hands;
>   you put everything under his feet:
> all flocks and herds,
>   and the beasts of the field,
> the birds of the air,

    and the fish of the sea,
    all that swim the paths of the seas.

O LORD, our LORD,
    how majestic is your name in all the earth!
(Psalm 8:1–9)

I learned from these two children a bit more of what Jesus meant when he called us to become like little children. I was reminded that gratitude and praise should just be normal conversation; that talking about God's truly awesome attributes (as shown by Jesus) is sometimes all that needs to be said; that when we think about what is true, noble, right, lovely, admirable, excellent, and praiseworthy (Philippians 4:8), joy exudes from within; and that singing and praying are what comes out of a heart in tune to God's love. Thanks, Lexi and Micah, for reminding me of the power of gratitude and praise. Try it and see if it doesn't help point you in a good and right direction.

another turkey at the door! 85

I am still smiling in disbelief over a little photo shoot that I experienced a few minutes ago. I had secretly prayed (and now it's no longer a secret) that I would get a new opportunity to photograph a turkey at a door, since the photo I'd taken of my original turkey-come-calling moment was fuzzy. I really wanted a great photo for this book. I realized, even as I prayed, that the odds of me witnessing a turkey showing up at another door were slim to none. However, I still carried my point-and-shoot camera in my purse—so I would be prepared, just in case it happened.

While I was driving home today, I spotted a turkey heading toward a house. After stopping my car in the road, I quietly emerged from the driver's seat, camera in hand. I tiptoed toward the turkey, ducking back and forth behind some stranger's parked truck so I could maneuver the turkey toward the door. I tiptoed; the turkey tiptoed, and...

Voilà! A turkey at the door! In fact, this turkey went to the back door *and* the front door.

I got back in my car grinning like a nut, thanking God for humoring my crazy prayer, and then I thought of the following scriptures about preparedness:

> If a man cleanses himself from the latter, he will be an instrument for noble purposes, made holy, useful to the Master and prepared to do any good work. (2 Timothy 2:21)
>
> Preach the Word; be prepared in season and out of season; correct, rebuke and encourage—with great patience and careful instruction. (2 Timothy 4:2)
>
> But in your hearts set apart Christ as Lord. Always be prepared to give an answer to everyone who asks you to give the reason for the hope that you have. But do this with gentleness and respect. (1 Peter 3:15)

I was convicted and inspired as I asked myself, How prepared am I to serve in any way at a moment's notice? How prepared am I to use the Bible in my relationships with others? How prepared am I to share my faith?

I certainly want to be even more prepared for these things than I was for the second turkey at the door! The stakes are incomparable. The opportunities to respond to all three of these questions are before me every day. Are you prepared for the "second turkeys" at your door?

the fellowship of those who encounter turkeys

86

I've been "up close and personal" with more turkeys than the average person. Besides the turkeys I've seen showing up on doorsteps, several years ago I also saw my neighbor jogging down the road by my house. At his heels was a turkey, which seemed set on attacking the man's sneakers. I'm sure it wasn't very Christian of me, but I couldn't help laugh as I observed my stick-wielding neighbor poke at the turkey that was in hot pursuit of his shoes.

Until I came up with the title for this book, I never knew that friends of mine had also had encounters with turkeys. When I shared the previous chapter, "Another Turkey at the Door," on my blog, a friend sent me a picture of a turkey she'd found at her door! Still another friend posted a picture of turkeys and a deer that she had encountered. Then yet another friend sent me a picture of a turkey perched atop her car! If that weren't enough, today a friend sent a picture of a turkey she found on her roof!

I'm not alone. All of us who have encountered turkeys have come to realize that they can be somewhat presumptuous, and even aggressive. So it is with the temptations and trials I face when I open my "life door" each new morning. Thankfully, I'm not alone in these encounters, either. There may be a small fellowship of "those who encounter turkeys," but there is a *universal* fellowship of those who face trials and temptations.

Take a look at these scriptures that address the idea of our shared struggles in Christ:

> Whatever happens, conduct yourselves in a manner worthy of the gospel of Christ. Then, whether I come and see you or only hear about you in my absence, I will know that you stand firm in one spirit, contending as one man for the faith of the gospel without being frightened in any way by those who oppose you. This is a sign to them that they will be destroyed, but that you will be saved—and that by God. For it has been granted to you on behalf of Christ not only to believe on him, but also to suffer for him, since you are going through the same struggle you saw I had, and now hear that I still have. (Philippians 1:27–30)

> If we are distressed, it is for your comfort and salvation; if we are comforted, it is for your comfort, which produces in you patient endurance of the same sufferings we suffer. (2 Corinthians 1:6)

> Resist him, standing firm in the faith, because you know that your brothers throughout the world are undergoing the same kind of sufferings. (1 Peter 5:9)

These scriptures remind me that:

- While we must take personal responsibility for standing firm in Christ and living in a manner worthy of his life and death, we can take comfort in knowing that other people have the same struggles we do.
- When I remember that my brothers and sisters in Christ

face and overcome trials and temptations, it helps me to also resist the similar temptations that Satan throws my way.
- When I receive comfort from people who have gone before me in trials, I am better able to patiently endure my own trials. When I overcome temptations and suffering, I become better equipped to help and comfort others.

The Bible encourages me, teaches me, and reminds me of how essential it is for us to be involved in each other's lives. God gave us the church for all those purposes. We need each other. I need to know I'm not alone, and I need the comfort, challenge, and encouragement of others who are also striving to live for God.

However, I am even more encouraged in knowing that not only does Jesus understand my weakness, but God's Spirit within me gives me the power to turn weakness to strength.

> Therefore, since we have a great high priest who has gone through the heavens, Jesus the Son of God, let us hold firmly to the faith we profess. For we do not have a high priest who is unable to sympathize with our weaknesses, but we have one who has been tempted in every way, just as we are—yet was without sin.
> (Hebrews 4:14–15)

I find inspiration and courage in claiming God's promise that with every temptation I face, I am also offered the power to overcome. Not only can I overcome, but God can turn my weaknesses into strengths.

> No temptation has seized you except what is common to man. And God is faithful; he will not let you be tempted beyond what you can bear. But when you are tempted, he will also provide a way out so that you can stand up under it. (1 Corinthians 10:13)

> To keep me from becoming conceited because of these surpassingly great revelations, there was given me a thorn in my flesh, a messenger of Satan, to torment me. Three

times I pleaded with the Lord to take it away from me. But he said to me, "My grace is sufficient for you, for my power is made perfect in weakness." Therefore I will boast all the more gladly about my weaknesses, so that Christ's power may rest on me. That is why, for Christ's sake, I delight in weaknesses, in insults, in hardships, in persecutions, in difficulties. For when I am weak, then I am strong.
(2 Corinthians 12:7–10)

May we use the Scriptures to guide our hearts and lives as daily we open our doors not just to turkeys, but also to opportunities, temptations, and the heavenly realm.

Made in the USA
Charleston, SC
03 October 2012